Road Connectivity and Development in Rural Mizoram

Road Connectivity and Development in Rural Mizoram

Lianhmingthanga

ANSHAH Anshah Publishing House

₹ 750 US$ 37.50
ISBN: 978-81-934379-7-1

First Published in India in 2018

Road Connectivity and Development in Rural Mizoram

Published by:
ANSHAH PUBLISHING HOUSE
LG 18-19, Pankaj Central Market
Patparganj, Delhi 110092
Ph. 011 22235152, 22235152
E-mail: info@shiprapublication.com
Website: www.shiprapublication.com

Preface

One of the most important catalysts credited to markedly spatial pattern of development of different economies is connectivity. Of the numerous connectivity infrastructures, road connectivity is often stated as the most fundamental and sought-after connectivity, particularly for rural areas, due to its flexibility and affordability within the community. At the same time, the increasing interest in rural development has brought with it an emphasis on the provision of rural infrastructure. Here, the construction and improvement of rural roads increasingly show potential for creating opportunities of economic growth and poverty reduction in developing countries.

The productivity of agriculture hinges largely on the efficiency in transportation which in turn is dependent on the level of road improvement. This creates vehicular operating benefits, transit benefits, and access benefits. Moreover, the provision of rural roads positively affects the demand of labour for men and women in farm and non-farm activities as well as larger investments in health and education for rural households in most remote areas. Rural roads also provide the important connectivity with growing markets adjacent to rural areas and also lessen input costs and transaction costs of rural producers and consumers. They are often a key spatial determinant of land use conversion as well. Better accessibility to agricultural lands or markets as a consequence of road connectivity allows farmers to reduce travel times and transportation costs to market towns, which confers substantial benefits on average, much of it going to poor households.

The north-eastern state of Mizoram was selected for the study. The state being land-locked, road transport is the principal means of communication for most community, business, and personal purposes. With slopes of hills ranging from 20° to 80° and an average elevation of 900 metres above sea level, the terrain of Mizoram does not permit easy accessibility to roads, and since road infrastructure is but a public good, there is no private investment in its provision in the state. At the same time, the state of Mizoram has a high performance in some demographic and socio-economic development variables like total literacy and female literacy rates, child sex ratio, and number of households with piped water supply, etc. However, its performance on key development parameters like employment rate and per capita income is comparatively low. Moreover, agricultural productivity is very low in the state and the market infrastructure is below par. It is thus an academic interest to study how road connectivity influences the development of the economy, and what the pattern of relationship is between rural road connectivity and development in the villages of Mizoram.

Although there are various factors at play that lead to spatial patterns of development set up across the different villages of Mizoram, the study observed clear distinction in the indicators of economic development among the villages that possess different connectivity status. In addition, taking the sign of the regression coefficient adopted in the exercise as the mode in which road connectivity impacted development (whether positively or negatively), it was found that road connectivity does have a direct bearing on economic development in the study areas.

Here, I want to thank the Mizoram Public Works Department, Rural Development Department, Directorate of Census Operations, Mizoram Remote Sensing Application Centre, Directorate of School Education, Health and Family Welfare Department, and Public Health Engineering Department for their cooperation during the stage of data collection.

I am indebted to Dr. James L.T. Thanga, Assistant Professor, Department of Economics, Mizoram University, without whom this work would not have been completed.

I also thank Dr. Lalhriatpuii, Assistant Professor, Department of Economics, Mizoram University, for all her help.

Also, I am grateful to my family and friends because I know that none of it would be possible without their love and patience.

Lianhmingthanga

Contents

List of Tables and Figure

Tables

Figure

List of Abbreviations

ADB – Asian Development Bank
ANOCOVA – Analysis of Covariance
AWR – All-Weather Roads
BMS – Basic Minimum Services
CAGR – Compound Annual Growth Rate
CHC – Community Health Centre
CI – Condition Index
CRF – Central Road Fund
CSS – Centrally Sponsored Scheme
DiD – Difference-in-Difference
EAS – Employment Assurance Scheme
FRDD – Fuzzy Regression Discontinuity Design
GDP – Gross Domestic Product
GIS – Geographic Information System
GoI – Government of India
HDI – Human Development Index
HMV – Heavy Motor Vehicle
IMR – Infant Mortality Rate
JNNURM – Jawaharlal Nehru National Urban Renewal Mission
JRY Jawahar Rozgar Yojana
LDCs – Less Developed Countries
LMV – Light Motor Vehicle
LPCD – Litres Per Capita Per Day
MIRSAC – Mizoram Remote Sensing Application Centre
MNP – Minimum Needs Programme
MoRD – Ministry of Rural Development
NABARD – National Bank for Agriculture and Rural Development
NEC – North Eastern Council
NESRIP – North Eastern State Roads Investment Programme
NH – National Highway

NITI	–	National Institute for Transforming India
NLCPR	–	Non-Lapsable Central Pool of Resources
NREP	–	National Rural Employment Programme
OBC	–	Other Backward Class
PCI	–	Per Capita Income
PHC	–	Primary Health Centre
PMGSY	–	Pradhan Mantri Gram Sadak Yojana
PRA	–	Participatory Rural Assessment
PWD	–	Public Works Department
RePEAT	–	Research on Poverty, Environment and Agricultural Technology
RLEGP	–	Rural Landless Employment Guarantee Programme
PQLI	–	Physical Quality of Life Index
SARDP	–	Special Accelerated Road Development Programme for North Eastern Region
SC	–	Scheduled Caste
ST	–	Scheduled Tribe
VLW	–	Village Level Worker

1

Introduction

Overview

It is a known fact that the development level of different economies varies immensely (Diener and Suh, 1997) and that an individual's chances of getting educated, finding a job, and escaping poverty largely depends upon the economy they are born in (Hull, 2009). These definitely hold true when viewed across countries, but there are also significant variations within countries. Although various factors are at play in this, one of the most important catalysts credited to the markedly spatial pattern of development is connectivity (Farole, 2012). Connectivity is considered to be the most important pre-requisite for human sustenance (Oraboune, 2008), and it includes communication networks through telephony, internet and postal services, electric connections, health infrastructure, educational infrastructure, and transport facilities through road networks (Sum, 2008). Among them, road connectivity is the most fundamental and sought-after connectivity, particularly for rural areas, due to its flexibility and affordability within the community.

The importance of roads and road transport has been recognised since the early times dating back to the Indus Valley Civilisation where streets were paved and the roads in the towns were straight and long, intersecting one another at right angles. With the advent of the Roman Empire, there was a need for armies to be able to travel quickly from one area to another and so, they built roads using deep roadbeds of crushed stone. Many roads were built throughout the Arab Empire as well. However, the first sophisticated roads paved with tar came to light in the eighth century in Baghdad, Iraq (Ajram, 1992). The nature and construction of roads gradually developed with the growth of the glamour of incessant struggle for mastery over the trade routes of the world. Contemporary asphalt roads capable of supporting vehicles emerged in the twentieth century and have undergone changes dramatically; going from large gangs of workers with picks and shovels to enormous specialised machines

(Abrams, 2013). Roads now have proved to yield a profound social significance. It is stated that if a community is primitive and stagnant, the inadequacy of their roads will indicate this fact and that economically advanced communities will necessarily possess an efficient and sufficient road system (Verma, 1980). As such, road connectivity has been viewed as one of the key components of national development, especially for a developing country in its drive for rural development.

Rural Development

The increasing interest in rural development is a result of the realisation that a systematic effort is necessary to create better living conditions in the rural areas where the vast majority of populations of developing countries reside. The term 'rural development' connotes overall development of rural areas to improve the quality of life of rural people (Chauhan, 2014). In this sense, it is a comprehensive and multidimensional concept, encompassing the development of agriculture and allied activities, village and cottage industries and crafts, socio-economic infrastructure, community services and facilities and, above all, human resources in rural areas. It has been defined in different ways. As a phenomenon, rural development is the end-result of interactions between various physical, technological, economic, social, cultural, and institutional factors. As a strategy, it is designed to improve the economic and social wellbeing of a specific group of people – the rural poor. As a discipline, it is multi-disciplinary in nature, representing an intersection of agriculture, social, behavioural, engineering, and management sciences (Singh, 2009).

Rural development has also been defined as a process of change by which the efforts of the people themselves are united with those of government authorities to improve their economic, social, and cultural conditions of communities to enable them to contribute fully to national programmes. Thus, it is a process of bringing change among rural community from the traditional way of living to a progressive way of living. It is also expressed as a movement for progress. Whatever be the differences in conceptualising the notion of rural development, there is a widely shared view that its essence should be poverty alleviation and distributive, justice-oriented economic transformation. So, the primary objectives of rural development includes – to improve the living standards by providing food, shelter, clothing, employment, and education; to increase productivity in rural areas and reduce poverty; to involve people in planning and development through their participation in decision making and through decentralisation of administration; and to ensure distributive justice and equalisation of opportunities in the society.

Therefore, rural development is a continuous process, which means that it is developmental and progressive and is primarily concerned with the optimum utilisation of resources – human, economic, social, and physical – in a given area through a systematic manner (Fajardo, 1994). This implies that rural development programmes should be well-planned, coordinated, and integrated. Also, the approach must be multi-sectored and planning should start from below. The target population should directly and actively participate in planning and in the implementation of development programmes. Moreover, although non-farm activities are also developed, the emphasis of rural development programmes has been agriculture development since most of rural population live and work in agriculture communities. It is concerned with not only the economic improvement of rural conditions but also other aspects that contribute to development of people and their quality of life. As such, rural development promotes a balanced development of all sectors in the rural areas.

Over the years, especially from the post-war era, rural development has become a matter of growing urgency. This is mainly for considerations of social justice, national integration, economic uplift, and inclusive growth (Chaudhary, 2012). It was found that rural development needs to complement urban development so that a balanced growth would be ensured and growth in each sector be mutually reinforcing. However, development of rural areas is constrained by a slew of factors such as lack of adequate employment opportunities and consequential rural-to-urban migration, frequent occurrence of drought and resultant loss of agricultural output and income, growing erosion of cropped area due to faster pace of urbanisation and industrialisation, dwindling water resources, and asymmetries and disparities in terms of economic and social indicators. Solutions to these issues lie in the reinvigoration of the agricultural sector, generation of gainful employment, creation of sufficient infrastructure in rural areas, thrust on a broad-based manufacturing sector, and strengthening of social services in rural areas.

Progress in rural development has also been hampered by structural and institutional biases against the rural poor. Emulating the relationship between the notions of 'core' and 'periphery' given by the dependency theory, there is a problem of 'urban bias' (Lipton, 2005) which, reduced to its bare essentials, puts forth the propositions that the development process in the developing countries is systematically biased against the rural areas and that this bias is deeply embedded in the political structure of these countries, dominated as they are by the urban groups (Varshney, 1998). So, there seems to be a systematic tendency for a country's resources to be unfairly and inefficiently distributed in favour of urban areas, to the detriment of people living in rural areas. At the same time, it is stated that rural roads represent the link between the urban 'core' and the rural 'periphery' (Windle and Cramb, 1997) and have the potential to counter some of the disadvantages of remoteness and provide benefits to all groups within a community.

Rural Road Connectivity

Rural infrastructure is a *sine qua non* for significantly improving the quality of human life and phenomenally accelerating the process of development; of which, the construction and improvement of rural roads increasingly show potential for creating opportunities of economic growth and poverty reduction in developing countries (Vargas, 2007). Rural roads may be defined as pure public goods (Ellis, 1997) as they have the characteristics of non-excludability and non-rivalry (Mankiw, 2014). This means that individuals cannot be effectively excluded from using the good and that an individual's use does not reduce the availability for others. In other words, the addition of an extra user does not reduce the supply for other users and there is no way to exclude others from using the good. Like that of other public goods, the market cannot play a significant role and thus, it has fallen on the government's shoulder to build and maintain rural roads. However, although private investment may not be suitable, there are a number of measures that can make provision of rural roads more responsive to the needs of the people. For example, if funds are diverted to the rural areas, local institutions may be more likely to be in tune with the demands of people and therefore prioritise infrastructural investment more efficiently and with less wastage (World Bank, 1994). Local level involvement at all levels of planning would increase commitment to the day-to-day maintenance required, the lack of which is probably the most common source of failure in infrastructural projects (Ellis, 1997).

Emphasis on farm marketing and procurement of farm supplies emerged with the commercialisation of farms and so, the productivity of agriculture hinges largely on the efficiency of transportation. This in turn is dependent on the level of road improvement which creates vehicular operating benefits, transit benefits, and access benefits (Singh, 1962). Moreover, the provision of rural roads positively affects the demand of labour for men and women in farm and non-farm activities as well as larger investments in health and education for rural households in most remote areas (Llanto, 2012). In villages with all-weather roads (AWR), not only do new and additional employment and business opportunities tend to increase (Golmohammadi, 2012) but also female wage employment (Lokshin and Yemtsov, 2005). Rural roads also provide an important connectivity with growing markets adjacent to rural areas and also lessen input costs and transaction costs of rural producers and consumers (Llanto, 2012). Rural roads are often a key spatial determinant of land use conversion (Ahmed et al., 2013).

Better accessibility to agricultural land or markets as a consequence of road connectivity can encourage people to convert lands (Munroe et al., 2004) while at the same time allows farmers to reduce travel time and transportation costs to market towns (Dorosh et al., 2009). This confers substantial benefits on average, much of it going to poor households (Jacoby, 2000). On the flipside, a deplorable state of rural roads affects the quality of farm produce and reduces cost of the product while at the same time reducing the quality of life and well-being of farmers (Ikejiofor and Ali, 2014). Additionally, an intense increase in road density creates favourable changes in land use and occupation (Freitas et al., 2009). With the development of roads, agricultural productivity tends to increase through expansion of crop production (Soares-Filho et al., 2004), and greater access to markets through rural roads may promote expansion of production into forest area and other fragile lands (Angelsen, 1999). In a nutshell, rural road improvements lead to substantial reduction in freight charges, increase in household income, more employment opportunities, and expansion of cultivated land.

In addition to these, connecting villages with all-weather roads increase the use of preventive health care by the residents and in these villages, women are more likely to seek antenatal care, to have delivery conducted by trained health personnel, and are more likely to use modern contraceptive methods (Banerjee and Sachdeva, 2015). It also leads to improvement in the accessibility to education facilities which results in increased school enrolment and school attendance, especially in the number of girls going to schools (Parida, 2014). Moreover, it bridges the gap between the enrolment of young men and women in secondary education, especially in rural areas (Bravo, 2002). Roads not only create physical pathways but also improve the informational connectivity between regions because increase in health care usage comes not only from increase in income or reduction in travel cost but also from increase in the awareness amongst households and individuals, improvement in health care supply, and increase in social interaction within and between villages, all of which have positive linkages with better road connectivity (Banerjee and Sachdeva, 2015).

The above arguments point to the notion that rural roads are an important factor that can bring about development especially for rural areas. They do not inherently favour the rural elite, satisfying the requirement of rural development strategies that benefit women, the most remote, and the most poor (Windle and Cramb, 1997). In that sense, this intervention has the potential to effectively reach a section of the population that has been persistently marginalised from the benefits of aggregate economic growth. While the availability and quality of rural infrastructure are never substitutes to efficient macroeconomic and agriculture-specific policies and the effective implementation of such policies, inadequate infrastructure can be a significant constraint to growth and productivity (Llanto, 2012). Therefore, rural road connectivity is viewed as a key component of rural development and a key ingredient in ensuring poverty reduction because it promotes access to economic and social services, thereby generating increased agricultural incomes and productive employment opportunities.

Overview of Existing Literature

Various studies of the field have been done in the past. Although such literatures vary greatly in methodology, in research objectives, and in temporal and spatial coverage, in most cases they support the hypothesis that rural road connectivity has favourable impacts on livelihood, production and productivity, poverty alleviation, and economic development in general.

The studies of Parida (2014), Ibok and Daniel (2013), Olagunju et al. (2012), Dorosh et al. (2011), Umoren et al. (2009), Mohapatra and Chandrasekhar (2007), Lombard and Coetzer (2006), and Windle and Cramb (1997) found a positive and significant relationship between road connectivity and economic development. Specifically, economic activities and employment opportunities increased with the provision of rural roads, thus leading to a reduction in poverty, according to the findings of Llanto (2012), Rasmussen and Broegaard (2011), Orabourne (2008), Khandker et al. (2006), and Lokshin and Yemstov (2005). Moreover, it was found in the works of Adedeji et al. (2014), Ikejoifor and Ali (2014), Kiprono and Matsumoto (2014), Eze (2012), Ulimwengu et al. (2009), and Mu and van de Walle (2007) that road connectivity does lead to agriculture development – its productivity and marketing; while Freitas et al. (2009) and Jacoby (2000) in particular found favourable changes in pattern of land utilisation as a result of the same.

In addition to these, reviewing of existing literature like the studies of Banerjee and Sachdeva (2015), Parida (2014), Golmohammadi (2012), and Castaing (2011) shed light on the fact that road connectivity does have significant impacts on the development of basic social infrastructures, specifically that of health and education. At the same time, the works of World Bank (2014), Atagher and Atagher (2014), and Bravo (2002) showed that improved rural roads have beneficial impacts on the women population. On the other hand, what has come to light from the review of various studies (World Bank, 2014; Golmohammadi 2012; Llanto, 2012; Khandker et al., 2006; Bravo, 2002; Windle and Cramb,

1997) is that road investments can contribute to spatial inequities across and within regions of better and poor connectivity statuses.

Some of the points that need to be addressed, but are scarce in the existing literature, are discussed in the following. Firstly, in their assessment, most studies took into account only the connectivity parameter of whether the study areas are connected with all-weather roads. They did not focus on road traffic. This means there is lack of analysis on if being frequented by vehicles on a daily basis plays a significant role in the development of that area. Moreover, in the majority of the literature, assessment was made by simply demarcating their study areas into connected and unconnected areas. No attempts were made to find out whether distance plays a distinctive role. Lastly, although deemed as a useful indicator of road infrastructure, only a handful considered density of road as a connectivity measure. It is important to account for the different levels of road density as this facilitates marketing and transport, thus having different economic returns and different impacts on economic development.

Current Situation of Road Connectivity in India

With a total road network of over 46,89,842 km, India has the second largest road network in the world. Moreover, the quantitative density of India's road network, represented by roads per square kilometre of land, is 0.66 km which is similar to that of the United States of America at 0.65. However, the quality of India's roads is a mix of modern highways and narrow, unpaved roads. Paved roads constitute only 54 per cent (NHDP, 2013). Roads in India are classified as Expressways, National Highways, State Highways, and rural and urban roads. Expressways, also known as Express Highways, are controlled-access highways, mostly 6-lane or above, where entrance and exit is controlled by the use of slip roads (ramps) that are incorporated into the design of the highway. On the other hand, National Highways are at-grade roads that connect various regions of one state to the other and are managed and maintained by agencies of the Government of India, while State Highways are usually roads that link important cities, towns, and district headquarters within the state and connect them with National Highways or highways of neighbouring states. State-wise, the national highway length per square kilometre ranges from 0.006 km for Jammu and Kashmir to 0.073 km for Goa, while the national average is 0.023 km. Moreover, the overall average of state highways per square kilometre is 0.05 with the highest being the state of Kerala at 0.112 km while Arunachal Pradesh does not have any (or negligible) state highway within its state (NITI Aayog, 2015).

Construction of rural roads is not a new phenomenon in India. Earlier, rural roads were seen as a means for revenue officials to reach the people for collecting land revenue, rather than for the benefit of the community. However, the construction of village roads was included under the Minimum Needs Programme (MNP) for the first time in the Fifth Five Year Plan (1974-79), which envisaged providing connectivity to population groups of 1500 persons or more with all-weather roads (All-weather roads, as its name suggests, are roads that are usable or operative in all kinds of weather). A definite outlay for this programme was made in each year for the Fifth Plan, though it decreased in the subsequent Five Year Plans. Further, the Government of India (GoI) initiated a number of programmes such as the National Rural Employment Programme (NREP) in 1980, the Rural Landless Employment Guarantee Programme (RLEGP) in 1983, the Jawahar Rozgar Yojana (JRY) in 1989, the Basic Minimum Services (BMS) in 1997, the Employment Assurance Scheme (EAS) in 1993, and other similar schemes under which rural roads were constructed year after year and plan after plan.

Notwithstanding the efforts made over the years at the state and central levels through different programmes, many habitations in the country are still unconnected by all-weather roads. Even where connectivity has been provided, the roads constructed are of such quality (due to poor construction or maintenance) that they cannot always be categorised as all-weather roads. Moreover, the rural roads sector is a state subject which lacks adequate planning and management due to poor coordination between multiple funding streams and agencies. Investing in rural roads was given low priority and viewed in isolation from the need for State and National Highways (World Bank, 2014). With a view to redressing the situation, the Government of India on 15 December 2000 launched Pradhan Mantri Gram Sadak Yojana (PMGSY) under the Ministry of Rural Development (MoRD) so as to provide all-weather access roads to unconnected habitations. The PMGSY is a 100% Centrally Sponsored Scheme (CSS) with the primary objective of providing connectivity, by way of all-weather road, to the eligible unconnected habitations in rural areas.

PMGSY initially envisaged the provision of new connectivity to about 180,000 habitations through the construction of about 372,000 km of roads, and upgrading about 370,000 km of the existing core rural network to provide full farm-to-market connectivity. This includes necessary culverts and cross-drainage structures that are operable throughout the year. The scheme aimed to cover all unconnected habitations with a population of 1000 persons and above within three years (2000-2003) and all unconnected habitations with a population of 500 persons and above by the end of the Tenth Plan Period (2007). In respect of the Hill States (North-East, Sikkim, Himachal Pradesh, Jammu & Kashmir,

Uttarakhand) and the Desert Areas (as identified in the Desert Development Programme) as well as the Tribal (Schedule V) areas, the objective was to connect habitations with a population of 250 persons and above. According to the latest figures made available by the State Governments under a survey to identify core network as part of the PMGSY programme, about 1.67 lakh unconnected habitations are eligible for coverage under the programme. This involves construction of about 3.71 lakh km of roads for new connectivity and 3.68 lakh km under upgradation.

The programme has greatly enhanced the capacity of states to plan and manage rural roads by the creation of state rural roads development agencies in each state. These agencies monitor PMGSY works, which are implemented by Public Works Departments (PWD), Rural Development departments, and similar agencies. This CSS, along with some State-run schemes, have had favourable effects on the life of Mizoram rural inhabitants as well.

Need for the Study

Road connectivity is a key component of rural development since it promotes access to economic and social services (MoRD, 2000), thereby generating increased agricultural productivity, non-agriculture employment, and non-agricultural productivity, which in turn expands rural growth opportunities and real income through which poverty can be reduced (Golmohammadi, 2012). The Indian state of Mizoram was selected for the study. As the state is land-locked, road transport is the principal means of communication for most community, business, and personal purposes. However, with slopes of hills ranging from 20° to 80° and an average elevation of 900 metres above sea level (Sawmliana and Roy, 2003), the terrain of Mizoram does not permit easy accessibility to roads, and since road infrastructure is but a public good, there is no private investment in its provision in the state.

At the same time, the state of Mizoram has high performance in some demographic and socio-economic development variables like total literacy and female literacy rates, child sex ratio and number of households with piped water supply, etc. However, its performance on key development parameters like employment rate and per capita income is comparatively low (NITI Aayog, 2015). Moreover, agricultural productivity is very low in the state and the market infrastructure is below par (Thanga, 2014).

It is thus an academic interest to study how road connectivity influences the development of the economy, and what the pattern of relationship is between rural road connectivity and development in the villages of Mizoram. It is believed

Table 1.1: Category-Wise Length of Roads: Mizoram (2013-14)

Sl. No.	Type of Roads	In Km			In Per cent		
		Surfaced	Un-surfaced	Total	Surfaced	Un-surfaced	Total
1	National Highways	986.530	0	986.530	100	0	100
2	State Highways	310.450	0	310.450	100	0	100
3	District Roads	1400.600	250.200	1650.800	84.84	15.16	100
4	Town Roads	253.202	44.204	297.406	85.14	14.86	100
5	Village Roads	948.061	1677.492	2625.553	36.11	63.89	100
6	Misc. Roads	877.980	799.310	1677.290	52.35	47.65	100
	Total	4776.823	2771.206	7548.029	63.29	36.71	100

Source: Mizoram Statistical Handbook, 2014

that the findings and suggestions of the study would bear substantial policy implications and assist policy makers in the production of blueprints for future programmes, particularly for those in relation to the goals of sustainability, universal coverage, and equity.

Rural Roads in Mizoram

The provision of rural roads in Mizoram is mostly undertaken by the State PWD and Rural Development Department. Although there has been a thrust of initiatives taken for the provision of rural roads in Mizoram, the situation is still at a distressing stage. The percentage of surfaced and unsurfaced roads in the state is given in Table 1.1.

The table shows that the total length of village roads in Mizoram, according to the Mizoram Statistical Handbook, 2014, is 2625.55 km, which constitutes 34.78 per cent of the total length of roads i.e. 7548.03 km. However, only 36.11 per cent of rural roads are surfaced while the remaining 63.89 per cent are fair weather roads. Moreover, at the time of the study, the percentage of villages connected with all-weather roads is 52.22 per cent. This means that 47.78 per cent of villages in Mizoram still have a deplorable status of connecting routes, let alone internal roads. In the district-wise analysis, it can be seen that while at least half of the villages in the districts of Mamit, Kolasib, Aizawl, Champhai, and Lunglei are AWR-connected, Serchhip, Lawngtlai, and Saiha districts have less than 50 per cent of their villages connected with all-weather roads. The district with highest percentage is Kolasib at 75.86 per cent while Saiha district has the lowest with only 28.57 per cent of its villages connected with AWR. This is shown in Table 1.2.

Table 1.2: Villages Connected with AWR

Sl. No.	Districts	Number of Villages			Percentage of Villages		
		Connected with AWR	Not Connected with AWR	Total	Connected with AWR	Not Connected with AWR	Total
1	Mamit	38	23	61	62.30	37.70	100
2	Kolasib	22	7	29	75.86	24.14	100
3	Aizawl	49	30	79	62.03	37.97	100
4	Champhai	38	38	76	50	50	100
5	Serchhip	12	19	31	38.71	61.29	100
6	Lunglei	55	52	107	51.40	48.60	100
7	Lawngtlai	46	53	99	46.46	53.54	100
8	Saiha	10	25	35	28.57	71.43	100
	Total	270	247	517	52.22	47.78	100

Source: Field Survey, 2015

On the other hand, more than half of the state's population lives in urban areas. Mizoram's population, according to the 2011 Population Census, is 10,91,014, of which 5,29,037 (48.49 per cent) are living in rural areas and 5,61,977 (51.52 per cent) are living in urban areas. This higher percentage of urban population is a distinguishing feature, making it one of the two states of India that possess a lower rural population relative to the total number of persons in the state, the other state being Goa. Moreover, during the past ten years (2001-2011), rural population increased by 81,470 and the urban population by 1,20,971 thus making the decadal growth rates in rural and urban areas 18.20 per cent and 27.43 per cent, respectively. The higher percentage of people currently living in urban areas may be cited as the effect of rural-urban migration, which is caused by multiple factors ranging from marriage and employment to lack of education and health facilities and lack of security in the rural areas (Essang and Mabawonku, 1975).

Therefore, looking at the status of village roads in Mizoram which is substandard and because it had been established by various researchers that rural roads bring about increased opportunities for employment and multiple socio-economic infrastructures, the construction and upgradation of rural roads is highly needed in the state to remove rural-urban dichotomy which would bring forth balanced development.

Methodology

A village level design was adopted; while the parameters and indicators assessed were road connectivity and economic development, which are further composed of a number of variables. So, the sampling unit of the study is a village, rather than individuals. It may be mentioned that different variables having diversified sources were used and as such, an explanation of the data variables is necessary while describing their sources. Detailed framework of data collection is enumerated in the following:

Study Area and Size

It is important to note that only the rural parts of the state are accounted for. As such, the urban areas – the state capital and the 23 notified towns – were excluded. The focus of the study is therefore on the 704 inhabited villages identified by the Population Census 2011. However, following the data of Geographic Information System (GIS) obtained from Mizoram Remote Sensing Application Centre (MIRSAC), some of the villages hypothesised to be having the same characteristics as they are located relatively closer to each other and the villages smaller in size and those with lesser population were merged with other villages, which made the total number of villages amount to 517. At the same time, it is important to note that the total population accounted for in the study is 5,25,435 which is the same as the total rural population of the 2011 Population Census. To explain this further, an example may be made of the Mamit district villages of Chilui, N. Sabual, N. Tlangkhang, Vawngawnzo, and Damdiai with respective populations of 102, 233, 80, 304, and 404, were merged and denoted in the study as Chilui with total population of 1,123. Another example is the merging of 12 villages of Lunglei District namely, Diplibagh, Serhuan, Nunsuri, Muriskata, Bindiasora, Thekaduar, Balungsuri, Zohmun, Silkur, Tiperaghat I, II, and III with populations of 1651, 551, 1,263, 206, 474, 316, 317 433, 278, 834, 554, 427 respectively, were represented by Diplibagh with total population of 7,304.

Connectivity Variables

Four sets of road connectivity variables were introduced in the study – whether the village is connected with AWR or not (in short, AWR Connectivity); whether it lies along or outside the main transport route of the state (Main Transport Route); distance of the unconnected village from the nearest AWR (Distance from AWR); and length of road network in the villages (Road Network).

a) *AWR Connectivity*: The Mizoram State Public Works Department was queried on the status of the 517 villages whether they are connected with AWR or not. However, for the information that could not be obtained from the same, the Village Councils were contacted telephonically and through letters regarding their status of connectivity. The data so obtained was then fitted to the respective villages thus showing qualitatively the connectivity status of the villages – those connected with AWR and those that are not. The study found the total number of connected villages to be 270 while 247 villages are not connected with AWR.

b) *Main Transport Route*: As it was felt that the status of the villages on AWR connectivity might fall short if not backed by regular road transport to that village, the parameter on whether it lies along the state's main transport route was earmarked as a connectivity variable as well. Here, 'main transport route' includes national highways, state highways, and roads connecting major transport destinations. The data for this variable was determined through interview of various stakeholders, particularly vehicle owners, transport operators, and knowledgeable persons. This again was vetted with the Department of Transport, Government of Mizoram for confidence. Thus, the key determinants on whether the villages are located along the main transport route or national highways, state highways, and the frequency of vehicles passing through the village. 112 villages were identified to be along the main transport route while the remaining 405 villages lie outside the route. A map displaying the roads identified as main transport routes in the study is given in Fig. 1.1.

c) *Distance from AWR*: As noted, the third parameter of road connectivity is the distance from the nearest AWR for those that are not connected with it. The data for this variable was obtained from two sources – the Public Works Department, Government of Mizoram and the Village Council of the villages, from which the bulk of it was procured from the latter. Here, the village councils that could be communicated through telephones were asked for the distance of their village from nearest AWR, while those that could not be contacted through telephones, were contacted through letters. The reported distances were then apportioned to the respective villages and thus accounted as a connectivity variable to check if distance of the village from AWR affects its development level.

d) *Road Network*: The data for the fourth variable adopted as a parameter of road connectivity i.e., length of the road network in the village was determined through the estimated area of the village within 1 km from motorable road obtained from the GIS data of MIRSAC. Technical assistance from a GIS expert was sought for working out this variable. The data obtained from

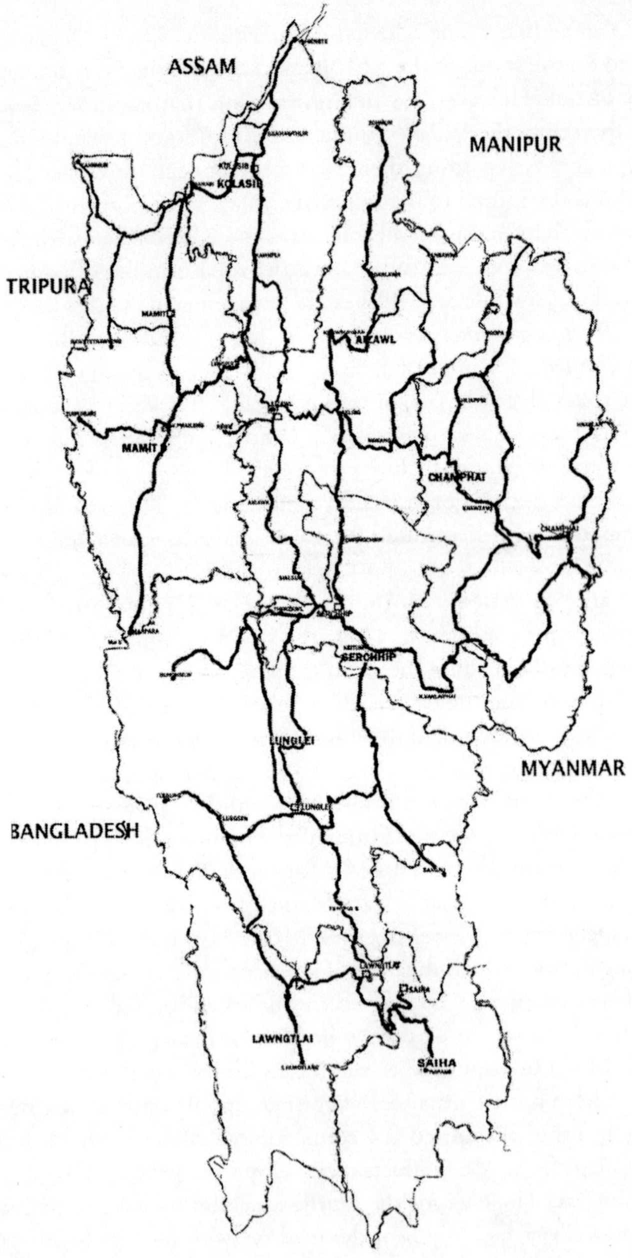

Figure 1.1: Map Showing the Main Transport Route of the State as Identified in the Study.

this source was later on allied with the data sets of the other connectivity variables to complete the road connectivity parameters of the study.

Development Indicators

The development indicators considered in the study can be broadly classified into four groups as well – population development, structure of employment, agriculture development, and basic social infrastructures. The variables used in each major development indicator and their sources are given as follows:

a) *Population Development*: The key variables used in the study under this head are mostly an indicator of population quality. They are sex ratio, child-population ratio, child sex ratio, family size, literacy rate, female literacy rate, and number of households in the villages. The data source for this indicator is the untabulated Primary Abstract of the 2011 Population Census obtained from the Directorate of Census Operations, Mizoram.
b) *Structure of Employment*: For studying the structure of employment, the variables taken into account are the percentage of workers to total village population, workers' sex ratio, percentage of main workers and marginal workers to total workers and the percentage of cultivators, agricultural labourers and household industry workers in both the main and marginal workers. These are also obtained from the Primary Abstract of Population Census 2011 through the Directorate of Census Operations, Mizoram.
c) *Agricultural Land Use*: Lack of detailed village data about land use precludes analysis of the impact of road connectivity on agricultural land use. Instead, the GIS data derived through satellite map as given by MIRSAC was used to represent the different statuses of land use of the villages. Here, the variables of interest are area of wet rice cultivation (WRC), agricultural plantation area, forest area—all represented as ratios to total area of the village—and average area under jhum cultivation per household denoted in hectares.
d) *Basic Social Infrastructures*: Under the social infrastructures are schools, water supply, and medical institutions. The number of schools, students, and teachers present in each of the villages of Mizoram was obtained from the 22 (twenty-two) Sub-Divisional Education Officers and 8 (eight) District Education Officers of the state. The number of schools was then added up for each merged village while the teacher-student ratio was calculated through the total number of students and teachers present in each village. At the same time, the amount of piped drinking water supplied to each village was obtained from the Public Health Engineering Department, Government of Mizoram. Here, the primary data of litres per

capita per day (LPCD) was computed and affixed for the villages. Lastly, for the number of health care institutions and the number of qualified medical personnel present in the villages, data was collected from offices of the 9 (nine) Chief Medical Officers across the state, which again was columned with the other development variables.

Analytical Tools

The primary and secondary data collected were analysed using suitable statistical tools. First, for testing the general trend of differences between the respective categories of the four connectivity variables, the study used descriptive statistics, namely, averages and percentages. Second, t-test and chi-square test were employed to test the significance of difference across villages of different road connectivity conditions i.e. to check whether there are significant differences in the development indicators of the study across the respective categories of the connectivity variables. The third statistical tool adopted is Dummy Variable Regression Model which was done so as to examine the pattern of relationship of differences across the road connectivity variables. The details of the second and third statistical tests are given in Chapter 4.

2

Situational Profile of Connectivity in India

Introduction

It is an academic interest to undertake an analysis of the status of road connectivity in the country as a whole so as to learn the present scenario which will guide us in the study of road connectivity and economic development for the study areas. As such, this chapter presents an overview of connectivity infrastructure and the level of socio-economic development of India and of Mizoram state, in particular. The status of connectivity infrastructures and socio-economic development of India was obtained mainly from the data of National Institute of Transforming India (NITI) Aayog. For Mizoram, the annual reports of the state Public Works Department (PWD), the various issues of Statistical Abstract and Economic Survey of Mizoram were being utilised.

The chapter is thus broadly divided into two parts. The first section shows the connectivity infrastructure of various states of India and their status of demographic and other socio-economic indicators of development. The second section focuses on the situational profile of road infrastructure in the state of Mizoram.

Connectivity Infrastructure and Socio-Economic Development Across the States of India

India has one of the largest road networks of over 48.65 lakh km, comprising of expressways, national highways, state highways, major district roads, other district roads, and village roads. The national highways with a total length of 96,214 km serve as the arterial network of the country (*Economic Survey*, 2014-15). The NITI Aayog's paper titled 'Comprehensive Roadmap for Development of North Eastern States....' identified six connectivity infrastructures, namely, highway length per sq. km, state highways per sq. km, per capita consumption of electricity presented in kWh, total rail route (km) per sq. km of area, percentage of rural tele-density, percentage of urban tele-density, and percentage of households electrified. At the same time, the indicators of socio-economic development are varied and comprise of literacy rate, infant mortality rate, child sex ratio, per capita income, households with improved drinking water, households availing banking services, among others. It would be important to note that the interpretation of the data of the following section covers just the extremes of each parameter while at the same time focusing on the North-Eastern States and Mizoram in particular.

Connectivity Infrastructures

The performance of the 28 states on the mentioned connectivity infrastructures is presented in Table 2.1. It can be seen that the highway length per square kilometre of the states ranges between 0.073 km and 0.006 km with an all India average of 0.023 km. In relation to the total geographical area of the state, Goa has the highest network of highways at 0.073 km while the national highway length of Jammu and Kashmir is the lowest at 0.006 km. There are 17 states above the national average and 10 states below it, while Karnataka stands at the average. Of the 17 states above the national average, six of the eight North-Eastern states are included. Mizoram with a length of 0.049 km has the fourth highest national highway network among the states of India.

At the same time, the state with the highest network of state highways per sq. km is Kerala at 0.112 km while Arunachal Pradesh showed 0 state highways. With the all-India average being 0.05, there are 13 states above this average of which five of the North-Eastern states fall short. Among them is Mizoram with a road network of 0.033 km which makes it the nineteenth state in terms of this connectivity infrastructure.

Table 2.1 also shows that the all-India average of total rail route per sq. km. of area is 0.02 km. There are 11 states which have rail route above the national average where Haryana stands first at 0.119 and Meghalaya and Sikkim at the bottom as the state is not connected with rail route. At the same time, Mizoram's rail route per sq. km of total geographical area is 0.0001 km which is the fifth lowest in the country.

In terms of per cent of rural tele-density, the highest percentage is Himachal Pradesh with 77.1 per cent and the lowest are Jharkhand and Bihar at 29.4 per cent. With an all-India average of 44 per cent, there are 11 states that have rural tele-density above this average. Mizoram has 42.7 per cent tele-density which

Table 2.1: Indian States in Terms of Connectivity Infrastructure

Sl. No.	States	Highway Length per sq. km.	State Highways per sq. km.	Total Rail Route (km) per sq. km. of Area	Rural Tele Density (%)	Urban Tele Density (%)	Household Electrified	Per Capita Consumption of Electricity (kWh)
	All India	0.023	0.05	0.02	44	145.5	67.2	914.4
1	Andhra Pradesh	0.016	0.039	0.018	45.4	167.6	92.2	1134.9
2	Arunachal Pradesh	0.024	0	0.00001	42.7	153	65.7	718.6
3	Assam	0.037	0.04	0.064	34.4	126.3	37	240.3
4	Bihar	0.044	0.052	0.026	29.4	151	16.4	145.4
5	Chhatisgarh	0.017	0.039	0.027	33.7	116.3	75.3	1495.4
6	Goa	0.073	0.075	0.049	72	154.3	96.9	2044.9
7	Gujarat	0.021	0.094	0.0004	57.4	137.6	90.4	1796.3
8	Haryana	0.037	0.057	0.119	59.8	121.4	90.5	1722.3
9	Himachal Pradesh	0.027	0.029	0.029	77.1	325.9	96.8	1379.8
10	Jammu and Kashmir	0.006	0.0003	0.001	42.6	130.7	85.1	1043.4
11	Jharkhand	0.027	0.024	0.003	29.4	151	45.8	846.8
12	Karnataka	0.023	0.108	0.011	46.2	167.2	90.6	1129.1
13	Kerala	0.037	0.112	0.083	64.3	189.7	94.4	630.1
14	Madhya Pradesh	0.016	0.034	0.003	33.7	116.3	67.1	752.7
15	Maharashtra	0.014	0.106	0.019	55.8	116.3	83.9	1239.3
16	Manipur	0.059	0.051	0.00004	42.7	153	68.3	352.9
17	Meghalaya	0.052	0.038	0	42.7	153	60.9	690.2

(Table 2.1 Continued)

(Table 2.1 Continued)

Sl. No.	States	Highway Length per sq. km.	State Highways per sq. km.	Total Rail Route (km) per sq. km. of Area	Rural Tele Density (%)	Urban Tele Density (%)	Household Electrified	Per Capita Consumption of Electricity (kWh)
18	Mizoram	0.049	0.033	0.0001	42.7	153	84.2	469.4
19	Nagaland	0.03	0.06	0.001	42.7	153	81.6	268.5
20	Odisha	0.024	0.023	0.016	39.9	161.1	43	1209.2
21	Punjab	0.031	0.029	0.044	72	154.3	96.6	1761.1
22	Rajasthan	0.021	0.031	0.017	48.6	160	67	981.9
23	Sikkim	0.021	0.025	0	42.7	153	92.5	861.8
24	Tamil Nadu	0.038	0.083	0.031	74	138.2	93.4	1226.3
25	Tripura	0.038	0.066	0.014	42.7	153	68.4	861.8
26	Uttar Pradesh	0.032	0.033	0.037	35.6	131.5	36.8	450
27	Uttarakhand	0.038	0.071	0.006	35.6	131.5	87	1297.3
28	West Bengal	0.03	0.051	0.045	41.7	135.3	54.5	593.9

Source: NITI Aayog, 2015

is the twelfth highest in the country. The scenario is slightly better for urban tele-density. With the all-India average at 145.5 per cent, there are 17 states above this average, including seven of the North-Eastern states. The highest position is occupied by Himachal Pradesh with 325.9 per cent while Maharashtra is at the lowest with 116.3 per cent. Mizoram is the ninth highest with 153 per cent which is the same percentage of urban tele-density of Arunachal Pradesh, Manipur, Meghalaya, Nagaland, Sikkim, and Tripura.

Moreover, the all-India average of electrified households stands at 67.2 per cent. There are 18 states with more electrified households than this average, including the North-Eastern states of Manipur, Mizoram, Nagaland, Sikkim, and Tripura. Goa has the highest number of its households electrified at 96.9 per cent and Bihar is at the bottom with 16.4 per cent. Mizoram has the thirteenth highest percentage in India at 84.2 per cent. Consumption of electricity is also presented in the table. Per capita consumption of electricity is lowest in Bihar at 145.4 kWh while it is highest in Goa with 2044.9 kWh. The number of states above the national average of 914.4 kWh is 14 – which is half of the total number of states in the country. With 469.4 kWh, Mizoram is among the states of low per capita consumption of electricity.

Socio-Economic Development

Table 2.2 shows the performance of the states on percentages of birth rate (2014), death rate (2014), unemployment rate (2011-12), and the total literacy rate (2011). Moreover, it also presents the infant mortality rate (per 1000 live births), percentage of underweight children under five years (2005-06), and child sex ratio (2011) denoted as number of females per 1000 males.

The all-India average birth rate is 21.4 per cent. There are eight states that have rates higher than this average among which the North-Eastern states of Assam and Meghalaya are included. Goa has the lowest birth rate at 13 per cent while the state with the highest birth rate is Bihar at 27.6 per cent. With 16.1 per cent, Mizoram is among the top ten states that have a low birth rate. The table also shows the death rate across the states of the country. It can be seen that there are eight states which have death rates equal to or greater than the all-India average of seven per cent. Here also, the state with the lowest death rate is Nagaland at 3.1 per cent while Odisha has the highest death rate at 8.4 per cent. Mizoram with 4.3 per cent has the third lowest death rate among the states of India.

The unemployment rate (2011-12) for India is 27 per 1000 population. There are 16 states having unemployment rates higher than this average including

Table 2.2: States on the Basis of Various Demographic and Socio-Economic Indicators

Sl. No.	States	Birth Rate (%) 2014	Death Rate (%) 2014	Unemployment Rate (per 1000) 2011-12	Total Literacy Rate (%) 2011	Gender Gap in Literacy (%) 2011	Infant Mortality Rate (per 1000 live births)	% of Underweight Children Under 5 Years (2005-06)	Child Sex Ratio (0-6 yrs) 2011
	All India	21.4	7	27	74	16.7	40	40.9	919
1	Andhra Pradesh	17.4	7.3	24	67.7	15.8	39	29.8	939
2	Arunachal Pradesh	19.3	5.8	21	67	14.1	32	29.7	972
3	Assam	22.8	7.8	50	73.2	11.5	54	35.8	962
4	Bihar	27.6	6.6	37	63.8	20.1	42	54.9	935
5	Chhatisgarh	24.4	7.9	20	71	20.9	46	47.8	969
6	Goa	13	6.6	48	87.4	11	9	21.3	942
7	Gujarat	20.8	6.5	7	79.3	16.5	36	41.1	890
8	Haryana	21.3	6.3	31	76.6	18.6	41	38.8	834
9	Himachal Pradesh	16	6.7	20	83.8	14.2	35	31.1	909
10	Jammu and Kashmir	17.5	5.3	48	68.7	20.3	37	24	862
11	Jharkhand	24.6	6.8	32	67.6	22.2	37	54.6	948
12	Karnataka	18.3	7	19	75.6	14.7	31	33.3	948
13	Kerala	14.7	6.9	91	93.9	4	12	21.2	964
14	Madhya Pradesh	26.3	8	11	70.6	20.5	54	57.9	918
15	Maharashtra	16.5	6.2	15	82.9	14.3	24	32.7	894

16	Manipur	14.7	4	47	79.9	13.3	10	19.5	936
17	Meghalaya	23.9	7.6	9	75.5	3.4	47	42.9	970
18	Mizoram	16.1	4.3	37	91.6	4.3	35	14.2	970
19	Nagaland	15.4	3.1	256	80.1	6.6	18	23.7	943
20	Odisha	19.6	8.4	29	73.5	18	51	39.5	941
21	Punjab	15.7	6.7	27	76.7	10.1	26	23.6	846
22	Rajasthan	25.6	6.5	17	67.1	27.9	47	36.8	888
23	Sikkim	17.1	5.2	11	82.2	10.9	22	17.3	957
24	Tamil Nadu	15.6	7.3	30	80.3	13	21	25.9	943
25	Tripura	13.7	4.7	146	87.8	9	26	35.2	957
26	Uttar Pradesh	27.2	7.7	24	69.7	20	50	41.6	902
27	Uttarakhand	18.2	6.1	42	79.6	17.6	32	31.7	890
28	West Bengal	16	6.4	44	77.1	11.5	31	37.6	956

Source: NITI Aayog, 2015

the North-Eastern states of Assam, Manipur, Mizoram, Nagaland, and Tripura. The state with the lowest unemployment rate is Gujarat in which seven per cent of the population is unemployed. The highest rate is suffered by Nagaland at 256 persons while the unemployment rate of Mizoram is 37 per 1000 which is the eighteenth lowest in India.

The all-India average for total literacy (2011) is 74 per cent. This rate is the highest in Kerala at 93.9 per cent while Bihar has the lowest literacy rate at 63.8 per cent. Mizoram comes second to Kerala at 91.6 per cent. Specifically, male literacy ranges between 96 per cent for Kerala and 73.4 per cent for Bihar. The national average is 82.1 per cent and Mizoram stands second with 93.7 per cent. On the other hand, female literacy rate ranges between 92 per cent for Kerala and 52.7 per cent for Rajasthan. The national average is 65.5 per cent and Mizoram proudly stands at the second place with 89.4 per cent. Therefore, it is evident that there is still a gender gap in literacy in the country which ranges from 3.4 per cent in Meghalaya to 27.9 per cent in Rajasthan. The literacy gender gap for Mizoram is 4.3 per cent while the all-India average stands at 16.7 per cent.

The national average for infant mortality rate (IMR) expressed as number of deaths per 1000 live births is 40. A close look at the table shows that there are nine states with infant mortality rate greater than this average, among which the states of Assam and Meghalaya are included. Goa has the lowest rate of infant mortality at nine while Madhya Pradesh and Assam have the highest rate of 54 per 1000 live births. For Mizoram, the infant mortality rate is 35 which is the fourteenth lowest in India. It can also be seen from the table that the child sex-ratio (0-6 years) ranges from 972 for Arunachal Pradesh to 834 for Haryana. Mizoram shares its position with Meghalaya and is the second highest in the country with 970. Moreover, with a national average of 919, there are 19 states with child sex ratio above this average, including all the eight North-Eastern states.

In addition to the above, it was felt that the analysis and interpretation should include data of per capita income (PCI), households with improved drinking water, households availing banking services, households with latrine, households with piped water supply, and percentage of rural population with piped water supply.

Table 2.3 shows that the percentage of rural household with access to improved source of drinking water is highest in Punjab at 99.5 per cent while it is lowest in Kerala at 29.5 per cent. Mizoram with 86.8 per cent is the sixteenth highest in India. Moreover, the data of urban households with access to improved source of drinking water shows that Himachal Pradesh has the highest percentage at 100 per cent while Kerala is the lowest at 56.8 per cent. Mizoram is the eighth highest at 99.1 per cent.

Table 2.3: States in Terms of Improved Source of Drinking Water, Banking, Latrine Facilities, Piped Water Supply and PCI

Sl. No.	States	% of HH With Improved Drinking Water (Rural)	% of HH With Improved Drinking Water (Urban)	HH availing Banking Services	HH with Latrine Within Premises	% of HH With Piped Water Supply (2014)	% of Rural Population With Piped Water Supply	Per Capita Income (2012-13) at 2004-05 Prices
1	Andhra Pradesh	91.9	97.5	53.1	49.6	14.64	67.09	44526
2	Arunachal Pradesh	96.2	98.4	53	62	2.21	55.08	35845
3	Assam	35.1	92.8	44.1	64.9	1.77	41.28	23448
4	Bihar	97.6	99.7	44.4	23.1	0.23	5.84	14362
5	Chhatisgarh	94.8	93.6	48.8	24.6	5.76	48.97	27421
6	Goa	33.9	99.6	86.8	79.7	0	0	132121
7	Gujarat	39.2	95.6	57.9	57.4	63.79	91.26	61220
8	Haryana	92.6	92.3	68.1	68.6	44.67	96.87	64136
9	Himachal Pradesh	95.8	100	89.1	69.1	23.3	92.91	51730
10	Jammu and Kashmir	30.6	97.9	70	51.2	48.35	84.46	29754
11	Jharkhand	64.4	88.3	54	22	1.01	21.41	27010
12	Karnataka	95.1	96	61.1	51.2	24.18	94.85	42976
13	Kerala	29.5	56.8	74.2	95.2	9.78	99.36	56115
14	Madhya Pradesh	83.2	97.1	46.6	28.8	8.03	28.74	25463
15	Maharashtra	85.5	98.7	68.9	53.1	33.43	82.32	64218
16	Manipur	57	69.8	29.6	89.3	2.79	93.47	22395
17	Meghalaya	70.4	94.5	37.5	62.9	0.72	76.35	34004

(Table 2.3 Continued)

(Table 2.3 Continued)

Sl. No.	States	% of HH With Improved Drinking Water (Rural)	% of HH With Improved Drinking Water (Urban)	HH availing Banking Services	HH with Latrine Within Premises	% of HH With Piped Water Supply (2014)	% of Rural Population With Piped Water Supply	Per Capita Income (2012-13) at 2004-05 Prices
18	Mizoram	86.8	99.1	54.9	91.9	3.66	97.02	39347
19	Nagaland	91.9	90.6	34.9	76.5	5.13	92.63	48111
20	Odisha	82.4	95.5	45	22	1.47	40.23	25415
21	Punjab	99.5	99.7	65.2	79.3	31.51	96.16	47834
22	Rajasthan	79.1	92.3	68	35	9.59	51.28	29244
23	Sikkim	85.2	98.8	67.5	87.2	42.86	100	78427
24	Tamil Nadu	94	95	52.5	48.3	20.08	93.96	58360
25	Tripura	87.3	99.7	79.2	86	1.37	80.44	42315
26	Uttar Pradesh	92.8	99.9	72	35.7	0	0.73	18595
27	Uttarakhand	96.6	99.2	80.7	65.8	13.36	68.98	54462
28	West Bengal	95	94.7	48.8	58.9	0.77	44.77	33889

Source: NITI Aayog, 2015

The table also shows that the percentage of households availing banking services is highest in Himachal Pradesh with 89.1 per cent and lowest in Manipur with 29.6 per cent while Mizoram is the fifteenth highest with 54.9 per cent. At the same time, the percentage of households with latrine facility within the premises is highest in Kerala with 95.2 per cent and lowest in Jharkhand and Odisha at 22 per cent. Mizoram has the second highest percentage at 91.9 per cent.

It can be computed that the national average for total households connected with piped water supply is 12.75 per cent, of which 10 states possess percentages higher than the average. The state with the highest percentage is Gujarat at 63.79 per cent while Goa and Uttar Pradesh have zero or negligible households connected with piped water supply. At the same time, Mizoram is the seventeenth highest with 3.66 per cent. Moreover, the national average for total rural population of states having access to piped water supply is 46.77 per cent. 20 of the 28 states have percentages higher than this average, including the North-Eastern states of Assam, Manipur, Meghalaya, Mizoram, Nagaland, and Tripura. On the all-India scene, Sikkim has the highest percentage with all of its households possessing piped water supply while Goa has no, or an insignificant number of, households with water supply. Mizoram is the third highest at 97.02 per cent.

States on the basis of per capita income (2012-13) at 2004-05 prices are also given in the table. Goa has the highest PCI at Rs. 1,32,121 while the state of Bihar has the lowest at Rs. 14,363. At the same time, Mizoram has the fifteenth highest PCI among the states with Rs. 39,347.

Road Connectivity Versus Socio-Economic Development

From the analysis of the connectivity infrastructures and the socio-economic development of the 28 states of India presented in the previous two sections, the following points can be derived:

First, accounting for the different levels of connectivity infrastructures present in the states, those that have infrastructures higher than the national average are also the ones that have higher than average performances in the various demographic and socio-economic development indicators. For example, among the 17 states that have literacy rates higher than the national average, 13 of the states have national highway lengths greater than the national average while 12 of the states have higher than average length of state highways. Here, it can be seen that Kerala, which has the highest network of state highways has the highest literacy rate in India. Moreover, 13 states and 11 states respectively of the 19 states that have lower than average IMR possess national and state highways higher than the national averages. It may be cited that Goa with the highest network of national highways has the lowest IMR in the country. In addition, 15 of the 18 states having child sex ratio higher than the national average have a higher than average highway length per sq km while the number of states that have state highway higher than the overall average among these is nine.

Second, the analysis of states on the basis of improved source of drinking water, banking, latrine facilities, and per capita income shows that majority of the states with higher than average performance in these indicators have connectivity infrastructures which are higher than the national average. An example may be cited of the states which have a percentage of rural households with improved drinking water that is higher than the national average. Here, 13 of the 18 states have total length of highways higher than the all-India average while 10 of these states have state highway infrastructure higher than the average. At the same time, in the analysis of the percentage of households with latrine facility within the premises, 14 of the 15 states that have percentages higher than the overall average possess a highway length that is longer than the national average while eight of them have state highway which is higher than the overall average. Moreover, among the 12 states that have the highest per capita income in the country, the percentage of states that have higher than all-India average lengths of both national and state highways is 66.67 per cent. Among them are Goa, which has the highest PCI and also the highest network of national highways, and Kerala, which has the highest network of state highways among the states of India.

In summary, it can be stated that states with developed connectivity infrastructures enjoy higher levels of development. This is evident by the analysis presented above where the majority of the states with better connectivity status have better performances on the socio-economic indicators of development. Therefore, it is safe to conclude that there is a close relationship between road connectivity and socio-economic development.

Road Connectivity Scenario in Mizoram

Being a hilly state with difficult terrain and climatic conditions, transport infrastructure in Mizoram is essentially road based. While there is a small metre-gauge rail link at Bairabi (about 130 km from Aizawl), an airport at Lengpui (44 km from Aizawl), for most community, business, and personal purposes, road transport is the only principal means of communication. However, the terrain of Mizoram does not permit easy accessibility to roads as the slopes of hills ranges from 20° to 80° and the average elevation is 900 metres above sea level. In clearer terms, the area within 1 km (say) from a motorable road does not necessarily mean that all the area within the perimeter is easily accessible because of its slope and elevation and the deep gorges between the hills. Therefore, it may be stated that construction and maintenance of roads should be and is a high priority in Mizoram, maybe even more so than the other parts of the country.

The roads of Mizoram are normally divided into five broad categories. They are:

i) *National Highways* (NH) which consists of NH-154 with a total length of 58 km connecting Bairabi to Bilkhawthlir; NH-150 of length 140 km which connects Seling to Manipur border; NH-44A of 130 km starting from Aizawl to Mamit to Tripura; NH-54A of 9 km connecting Hrangchalkawn and Lunglei; NH-54B of length 27 km which connects Zero Point and Saiha; NH-54 of 522 km starting from Lailapur to Tuipang; and NH-502A with a total length of 100 km which is a multi-modal road, i.e. NH-54 at Lawngtlai to Myanmar border.
ii) *State Highways* which connect the other district capitals not connected by the national highways.
iii) *Town roads* within the 23 notified towns of the state.
iv) *Village roads* which consist of both approach and internal link roads of the villages.
v) *Miscellaneous roads* which are the other roads of the state that do not fall under the previous four categories.

Total Length of Roads in Mizoram

As per the Mizoram State Road Statistics 2014, the total length of all types of roads in Mizoram as on 2014 is 7548.03 km and road density is 35.50 km/100 sq. km. The road density in Mizoram is still relatively low when compared to the average national level road density of 129.00 km/100 sq. km.

The category-wise length of roads in Mizoram is shown in Table 2.4 where 4776.82 km out of the total length of roads in Mizoram is surfaced while the remaining is not. It would be important to note that the national and state highways of the state are represented as surfaced although some of the national highways are being reported as 'unsurfaced'. It is hypothesised that this is because of wear and tear after being initially surfaced and so, the present study considered all of the highways to be surfaced.

Table 2.4 further shows that 1400.6 km out of the total district roads of 1650.8 km is surfaced while for the town roads, the length of surfaced roads total to 253.202 km. The worst situation is suffered by village roads where the total length is 2625.55 km of which only 984.06 are surfaced.

In order to present the length of surfaced roads in clearer terms, the district-wise breakup of the various types of roads is presented in percentages in Table 2.5. It may be noted that since a more recent one is not available, the data

Table 2.4: Total Length of Surfaced and Unsurfaced Roads in Mizoram

(in km)

Sl. No.	Type of Roads	Surfaced	Unsurfaced	Total	Density
1	National Highways	986.530	0	986.530	4.68
2	State Highways	310.450	0	310.450	1.47
3	District Roads	1400.600	250.200	1650.800	7.83
4	Town Roads	253.202	44.204	297.406	1.50
5	Village Roads	948.061	1677.492	2625.553	12.45
6	Misc. Roads	877.980	799.310	1677.290	7.57
Total		4776.823	2771.206	7548.029	35.50

Source: Mizoram Statistical Handbook, 2014

Table 2.5: Percentage of Surfaced Roads in Mizoram: District-Wise

in percentages

Sl. No.	District	National Highway	State Highway	District Road	Village Road	Town Road	Total
1	Mamit	100	100	69.40	15.09	64.15	75.87
2	Kolasib	100	100	58.64	25.27	57.42	72.67
3	Aizawl	100	100	60.14	23.85	80.58	74.17
4	Champhai	NA	100	69.30	20.57	67.80	66.88
5	Serchhip	100	100	54.60	13.41	62.41	71.35
6	Lunglei	100	100	50.80	-	75.60	65.88
7	Lawngtlai	100	100	44.46	11.31	26.16	56.50
8	Saiha	100	100	9.88	-	92.02	50.63
	Total	100	100	54.19	15.75	71.73	67.38

– Data not available

Source: Statistical Abstract of Mizoram: 2013

given in the Statistical Abstract of Mizoram: 2013 is being used and so, the data is subject to change within the past years. However, it is believed that it would represent the existing status to a great extent. Moreover, the national highways and state highways are being presented here as 'surfaced'. The reasoning of which has already been given.

The total percentage of surfaced roads in the state is 54.19 per cent for district roads and 15.75 per cent for village roads. The town roads show a relatively favourable situation as 71.73 per cent are surfaced. Saiha district has the worst situation for districts roads with only 9.88 per cent of them being surfaced while Mamit has the highest percentage at 69.40. It can also be seen from the table that the percentages of village roads that are surfaced are very low, ranging from 11.31 per cent for Lawngtlai to 25.27 per cent for Kolasib. At the same time, the roads of the 23 towns of the states are much better than these two types of roads although there are stark differences among the districts. Saiha district has surfaced town roads of 92.02 per cent but for Lawngtlai, the percentage is only 26.16.

Progressive Number of Vehicles on Road

As the provision of roads is synonymous with transport, it was considered necessary to analyse the increasing rate of vehicles in the state. The year-wise data for the number of different types of vehicles on road is given in Table 2.6. It should be noted here that light motor vehicles (LMVs) consist of motor cabs, maxi cabs, motor cars and the like while heavy motor vehicles (HMVs) are trucks, tractors, trailers, etc. Under the 'Others' category are ambulances, fire fighters and recovery vans, among others.

It can be seen from the table that the number of registered vehicles keeps on increasing with the passage of time. There were 14,182 additional vehicles during the years 2010-11 and 2011-12 while for the next year, i.e. 2012-13, the number of registered vehicles increased to 1,21,330. In 2013-14, there were a total of 1,37,225 registered vehicles which is an increase by 15,895 vehicles from the previous year (2012-13). The table also shows that the computed compound annual growth rate (CAGR) of all types of vehicles is 14.22 per cent where the highest growth rate was experienced in the number of three-wheelers which grew at the rate of 20.32 per cent annually while the number of two-wheelers grew at 16.53 per cent per annum over the period of four years.

Table 2.6: Number of Vehicles on Road

Sl. No.	Types	2010-11	2011-12	2012-13	2013-14	CAGR (%)
1	Two Wheeler	50898	60278	70449	80729	16.53
2	Three Wheeler	2544	3029	3669	4425	20.32
3	LMV	32475	36126	40021	44318	10.85
4	HMV	5285	5796	6199	6596	7.57
5	Others	721	876	992	1157	16.65
	Total	91923	106105	121330	137225	14.22

Source: Statistical Handbook (various issues), Govt. of Mizoram

Public Expenditure on Roads and Road Transport

The funding of road upgradation and maintenance programmes of the Public Works Department (PWD) depend mainly on State and Central Government allocations. Table 2.7 presents the analysis of the annual expenditure for roads and transport under plan scheme in Mizoram during the past ten years.

It is shown in the table that the sub-heads of 'Roads and Bridges' and 'Road Transport' taken together constitute almost all of the annual expenditure allocated for the head 'Transport' in every year of the presented ten years. The percentages range from 93.61 per cent in 2007-08 to 99.29 per cent in 2005-06; while for 2013-14, it is 94.57 per cent of the total amount allocated for transport. This dedication of the budget expenditure shows that road and its transport are considered the most important means of transport communication in the state. In absolute terms, the amount of expenditure for the two sub-heads is Rs. 142.92 crore in 2007-08 and Rs. 51.23 crore 2008-09; while in 2013-14, it is Rs. 83.03 crore which is higher than the amount in 2012-13 at Rs. 74.33 crore. Taking the total plan budget of the state into account, the percentage of total road and road transport taken together accounted for 4.71 per cent in 2013-14. It was as high as 18.94 per cent in 2005-06 and 18.39 per cent in 2007-08, and sank to 4.27 per cent in 2012-13.

The calculated CAGR of expenditures on total road and bridges summed with total transport turned out to be –3.73 per cent while that of the transport head is –3.53 per cent. On the other hand, the total plan budget increased at the rate of 14.45 per cent per annum during the last ten years. This means that while the amount of expenditure of the total plan budget has been on the rise, the amount allocated and spent for the 'Transport' head as a whole and total of 'Road and Bridges' and 'Road Transport' in particular experienced a falling trend.

Since road transport is the major mode of transport within the state, improvement of road network is believed to be the major key to achieve development in the state as better connectivity enhances the environment for development and growth by reducing freight and passenger transport costs, and by providing quicker and safer access to all parts of the state and to neighbouring state and countries thereby promoting tourism in the state. Moreover, as the major occupation of the people is agriculture, easy access to remote, hilly, mountainous regions and low lying areas would cause increased agricultural produce in the state. Therefore, it is a priority of the state government and the Mizoram PWD in particular to spurge up the status of roads.

Concluding Remarks

An overview of the scenario of connectivity and socio-economic development across the country shows a positive relationship between the availability of connectivity infrastructure and socio-economic development. This is evident from

Table 2.7: Annual Expenditure for Roads and Transport Under Plan Scheme

Rs. in Crore Unless Specified Otherwise

Sl	Heads	2004-2005	2005-2006	2006-2007	2007-2008	2008-2009	2009-2010	2010-2011	2011-2012	2012-2013	2013-2014
1	Transport										
	a) Aviation	0.00	0.07	0.29	0.82	2.27	0.67	1.25	0.86	1.43	3.71
	b) Roads and Bridges	89.74	126.47	112.61	138.62	47.26	66.49	125.34	85.85	70.00	78.38
	c) Road Transport	4.00	4.71	4.95	4.30	3.97	6.01	5.00	4.99	4.33	4.64
	d) Inland Water Trans.	0.05	0.05	0.32	0.04	0.04	0.05	0.04	0.05	0.05	0.05
	e) M.V. Wing	0.77	0.82	1.01	1.15	1.01	0.93	1.06	1.09	0.84	1.01
2	Total Road (b + c)	93.74	131.18	117.56	142.92	51.23	72.50	130.34	90.84	74.33	83.02
3	Total Transport (a to e)	98.56	132.12	119.18	144.93	54.55	74.15	132.69	92.84	76.65	87.79
4	Total Plan Budget	550.40	692.64	745.32	777.13	839.29	1152.75	1288.69	1534.82	1741.74	1762.62
5	% of Total Road in Total Transport	95.11	99.29	98.64	98.61	93.91	97.77	98.23	97.85	96.97	94.57
6	% of Total Road in Total Budget	17.03	18.94	15.77	18.39	6.10	6.29	10.11	5.92	4.27	4.71

CAGR: a) Total Road = - 3.73%, b) Total Transport: - 3.53%, c) Total Plan Budget: 14.45%

Source: Economic Survey (various issues). Govt. of Mizoram

the fact that most of the states above the national average in terms of connectivity infrastructure are also above the national average in socio-economic development status. The state of Mizoram has commendable achievements in terms of connectivity for being above the national average and at the same time, having higher than average achievements in human development like literacy, child sex ratio, etc. However, it shows comparatively poor performance on unemployment rate and per capita income.

Although the state of Mizoram is among the top five in the country with regard to the measure of National Highway density, it still shows a relatively low road density within the state. This may be construed as the poor performance of the state in constructing road connectivity infrastructure on its own. Of the eight districts, those in the northern parts of the state are showing better road conditions as they have higher percentages of surfaced roads. At the same time, the percentages of southern districts are well below the northern districts, which indicate unequal regional development of the state on road infrastructure. Another notable feature on the status of road connectivity in the state is the extremely poor status of village roads – the main transport infrastructure for the rural population. Moreover, the condition of town roads is no better. Taking into account the high increasing rate of vehicles plying on the road side by side with the high unsurfaced roads, it means that a large number of vehicles are regularly plying on the poor unsurfaced village and town roads. This would cause the vehicles owners as well as commuters to exhaust huge expenses in their movement from one place to another, the reason for which may be social or political, but mostly economic.

3

Existing Status of Rural Road Connectivity and Economic Development in Mizoram

Introduction

The provision of road connectivity has a positive relation with economic development of both urban and rural areas. For rural areas in particular, it brings forth multiple socio-economic benefits which form a strong base for the economy and is a powerful instrument for the socio-economic transformation (Lombard and Coetzer, 2006). Therefore, roads are among the most important public assets because they bring immediate benefits to road users through improved access to hospitals, schools, and markets, thereby enhancing comfort, speed, and safety. In communities where there is access to extended networks of transport infrastructure, markets are more likely to be developed (Mu and van de Walle, 2007) and benefits from improving access to basic education depend on such investments in infrastructure (Deininger and Okidi, 2003).

Moreover, road improvements lead to lower input and transportation costs, higher production, higher wages, and higher output prices (Khandker et al., 2006) while raising the productive capacity of poor households as well (Jacoby, 2000). Road connectivity not only affects the agricultural sector but also increases opportunities for off-farm and female wage employment (Lokshin and Yemtsov, 2005).

This chapter presents the analysis of the impact of rural road connectivity on economic development of the villages of Mizoram. This has been done by checking whether there are differences in levels of development when their status of connectivity is being accounted for. In other words, this chapter attempts to demonstrate the effect that the status of village road connectivity has on the level of development by identifying performance variations in selected parameters of development across different connectivity measures. It may again be mentioned that the study focuses only on the rural parts of the state.

The chapter is divided into two broad sub-chapters. First, it discusses in detail the various measures of road connectivity used in the study and second, it shows the tests of relationship between the connectivity measures and development variables. The connectivity parameters employed were:

1) whether the village is connected with all-weather road (AWR);
2) whether it lies along the main transport route;
3) the locational distance of the village from the nearest all-weather road; and
4) the village's road network derived from the area of village within 1 km from motorable road.

As stated, the latter part of the chapter shows the analysis of the study area using these road connectivity measures to determine the development status of the villages through different parameters and to check whether there are distinctions between the categories of each set of classifications. The development parameters used were basic population characteristics, economic activities of the population, agriculture land use, and basic socio-economic parameters like education and health care, etc.

Classification of Villages

The selected 517 villages were classified according to the mentioned connectivity measures. The first classification was done by taking into account whether the village is connected with an all-weather road or not. The primary data for this classification was obtained from the Public Works Department, Government of Mizoram in raw form. However, for the information that cannot be obtained from the same, the Village Councils were contacted through letters and telephonic enquiries of their status of connectivity. The villages were then fitted their respective connectivity status and then grouped into those connected with AWR and those that are not.

Table 3.1 shows that in total, more than half (52.22 per cent) of the villages in Mizoram are connected with all-weather roads (AWR). In the district-wise analysis, it can be seen that while at least half of the villages in the districts of Mamit, Kolasib, Aizawl, Champhai, and Lunglei are AWR-connected, Serchhip, Lawngtlai, and Saiha districts have less than 50 per cent of their villages connected with all-weather roads. It can also be seen that the district with the highest percentage of connectivity is Kolasib at 75.86 per cent while Saiha district has the lowest, with only 28.57 per cent of its villages connected with AWR.

The second classification was determined through an examination of whether the village lies along the main transport route on which vehicles ply

Table 3.1: Villages with AWR Connectivity

Sl. No.	Districts	Number of Villages			Percentage of Villages		
		Connected with AWR	Not Connected with AWR	Total	Connected with AWR	Not Connected with AWR	Total
1	Mamit	38	23	61	62.30	37.70	100
2	Kolasib	22	7	29	75.86	24.14	100
3	Aizawl	49	30	79	62.03	37.97	100
4	Champhai	38	38	76	50	50	100
5	Serchhip	12	19	31	38.71	61.29	100
6	Lunglei	55	52	107	51.40	48.60	100
7	Lawngtlai	46	53	99	46.46	53.54	100
8	Saiha	10	25	35	28.57	71.43	100
	Total	270	247	517	52.22	47.78	100

Source: Field Survey, 2015

on a daily basis. The data for it was acquired through an interview with various stakeholders, particularly vehicle owners, transport operators, and knowledgeable persons. This again was cross-checked with the Department of Transport, Government of Mizoram for confirmation. The 'main transport route' in the study includes the national highways, state highways, and roads connecting major transport destinations. This classification may be justified as mere connectivity like that of the first classification may not translate into development if transport to that village is irregular and uncertain. The district-wise scenario is given in Table 3.2.

It can be seen from the table that 21.66 per cent of Mizoram villages are being passed through by the main transport routes. Here, Aizawl district ranks the highest as 44.30 per cent of its villages are lying along the main route. While four districts (Mamit, Kolasib, Aizawl, and Lunglei) have percentages above the state average, Lawngtlai district is the lowest with only 6.06 per cent of its total villages lying along the major transport route of the state. Moreover, the table also shows that districts of Saiha (11.43 per cent), Champhai (10.53 per cent), and Serchhip (16.13 per cent) have percentages lower than the state average.

To check if distance of the village from AWR plays a role in development, data was obtained from the Village Council of the villages and Public Works Department, Government of Mizoram. Therefore, the third classification focused on the villages that fall under 'not connected with AWR' of the first classification. Here, the bulk of the information was acquired from the village

Table 3.2: Villages Along Main Transport Route

Sl. No.	Districts	Number of Villages			Percentage of Villages		
		Along Main Route	Outside Main Route	Total	Along Main Route	Outside Main Route	Total
1	Mamit	20	41	61	32.79	67.21	100
2	Kolasib	7	22	29	24.14	75.86	100
3	Aizawl	35	44	79	44.30	55.70	100
4	Champhai	8	68	76	10.53	89.47	100
5	Serchhip	5	26	31	16.13	83.87	100
6	Lunglei	27	80	107	25.23	74.77	100
7	Lawngtlai	6	93	99	6.06	93.94	100
8	Saiha	4	31	35	11.43	88.57	100
	Total	112	405	517	21.66	78.34	100

Source: Field Survey, 2015

councils through telephones and through letters. They were asked the distance of their village from the nearest AWR and the reported distances were then apportioned to the respective villages. The villages were grouped into those that are within 15 km and outside 15 km of the nearest AWR.

Thus, this classification divides the study area into three categories – those connected with AWR, those within 15 km of AWR and those farther than 15 km from the nearest AWR. Simply put, the first category of the classification would automatically be made up of the 270 villages connected with AWR, while the remaining 248 are divided into villages within and outside 15 km of the nearest AWR. As already stated, the villages of the second and third categories (i.e. those not connected with AWR) will be the focus in the immediate and subsequent interpretation. Table 3.3 shows the classification of the study area according to their distance from the nearest AWR.

As is already shown under Classification I, the percentage of villages connected with all-weather road is 52.22 per cent. Among those that are not, 25.53 per cent are within 15 km of the nearest AWR while 22.24 per cent are outside i.e. farther than 15 km. Here, the situation is worst in Saiha district as 57.14 per cent of its villages are more than 15 km away from the nearest AWR. The situation is also acute in Serchhip district at 41.94 per cent, while Lunglei district with 24.30 per cent is also higher than the state average.

The table also shows that in the district of Kolasib, all of its villages are within 15 km of the nearest AWR, if not connected with it. Mamit district also shows a heartening situation as only 6.56 per cent of its villages are more than

Table 3.3: Distance of Villages from the Nearest AWR

Sl. No.	Districts	Number of Villages				Percentage of Villages			
		AWR	Within 15 km	Outside 15 km	Total	AWR	Within 15 km	Outside 15 km	Total
1	Mamit	38	19	4	61	62.30	31.15	6.56	100
2	Kolasib	22	7	0	29	75.86	24.14	0	100
3	Aizawl	49	15	15	79	62.03	18.99	18.99	100
4	Champhai	38	22	16	76	50	28.95	21.05	100
5	Serchhip	12	6	13	31	38.71	19.35	41.94	100
6	Lunglei	55	26	26	107	51.40	24.30	24.30	100
7	Lawngtlai	46	32	21	99	46.46	32.32	21.21	100
8	Saiha	10	5	20	35	28.57	14.29	57.14	100
	Total	270	132	115	517	52.22	25.53	22.24	100

Source: Field Survey, 2015

15 km away from the nearest AWR while 31.15 are within 15 km. It can also be seen that in Aizawl district, the percentage of villages 'within' and 'outside' are the same at 18.99 per cent. In Lawngtlai district, the percentage of villages within 15 km is 32.32 while 21.21 per cent are farther than 15 km from AWR. Moreover, the percentages are 28.95 and 21.05 for villages within and outside 15 km of nearest AWR for Champhai district.

Lastly, the fourth classification accounted the total road network present in each village. This was done by determining the area of the villages within 1000m from motorable road; which was generated from the road network data of Mizoram Remote Sensing Application Centre (MIRSAC). The motorable road here encompasses a wide denotation as it includes National Highways, State Highways, District Roads, and Village Roads. The villages are then divided into two categories – those with road network 'below' and 'above' 7.5 km.

Table 3.4 shows that in Mizoram, 41.20 per cent of villages have road network above 7.5 km while 58.80 per cent are with road network below 7.5 km. This means that road network is still low in spite of the fact that more than half of the villages are connected with all-weather roads.

The district with the highest percentage of its villages falling under 'Above 7.5 km' is Kolasib with 72.41 per cent followed by Mamit district with 65.57 per cent. The other two districts with percentages higher than the state average are Champhai (52.63 per cent) and Lunglei (45.79 per cent). It can also be seen that the overall percentage is being pulled down by the low densities of road in villages of Lawngtlai (13.13 per cent) and Saiha (20 per cent) districts while

Table 3.4: Road Network of Villages

Sl. No.	Districts	Number of Villages			Percentage of Villages		
		Below 7.5 km	Above 7.5 km	Total	Below 7.5 km	Above 7.5 km	Total
1	Mamit	21	40	61	34.43	65.57	100
2	Kolasib	8	21	29	27.59	72.41	100
3	Aizawl	48	31	79	60.76	39.24	100
4	Champhai	36	40	76	47.37	52.63	100
5	Serchhip	19	12	31	61.29	38.71	100
6	Lunglei	58	49	107	54.21	45.79	100
7	Lawngtlai	86	13	99	86.87	13.13	100
8	Saiha	28	7	35	80.00	20.00	100
	Total	304	213	517	58.80	41.20	100

Source: Mizoram Remote Sensing Application Centre, 2014

Serchhip (38.71 per cent) and Aizawl (38.24 per cent) districts are also below the state average.

Road Connectivity and Rural Development in Mizoram

As mentioned in the introductory part of this chapter, the previously enumerated classifications of road connectivity were used as independent variables for analysing the development status of the study areas. Although varied and numbered development parameters had been specified by different studies, the present study selected and focused on certain parameters available in the state.

First, it was tested whether the different classifications of road connectivity had impacts on the population characteristics like sex ratio, child sex ratio, literacy rate, and the density of population, among others.

Second, it was analysed whether there were differences within the categories of the four classifications when the workers' details such as number of workers, main workers and marginal workers of the villages were taken into account.

Third, the land-use data like area of wet rice cultivation, plantation, forest cover and jhum cultivation were determined and it was checked if the villages' status of road connectivity had any impact on them.

Last, the four classifications of road connectivity were tested on the basis of social infrastructures namely, educational institutions, health care facilities, and water supply.

Population Status

One of the simplest ways in which the development of an economy can be judged is by its demography because it is acknowledged as the single most important supply-side determinant of economic activity and employment trends especially in rural areas (Copus et al., 2006). Moreover, the current view of development is that the variables—development and population—are inseparable, and that the explanation of trends for one of these cannot be sought in isolation from the other (Mostert, 1985). Therefore, it is interesting to examine whether road connectivity has impacts on the population structure of the study area. The selected variables under this parameter includes total population, sex ratio, population of children below six years, child sex ratio, male and female literacy rates, number of households, family size, and population density – all taken in averages and checked using the four classifications discussed at length in the previous section.

Table 3.5 and 3.6 show the selected population characteristics of the study areas with the mentioned classifications, viz., connectivity status and whether they are along main transport route, and distance from nearest AWR and the network of road in the villages.

First is the total population of the villages. This is important because population modifies the man-land ratio, facilitates specialisation, and communication, and provides other economies of scale (Boserup, 1976). The study of the impact of road connectivity on population has been done by Dorosh et al. (2012) and is also accounted for in the various impact assessments of Pradhan Mantri Gram Sadak Yojana (PMGSY) in different states of India.

As can be seen in the table, the classification of villages into those that are connected and not connected with AWR shows that the number of people living in villages connected with AWR is significantly higher than in those that are not. Here, the average person per village is 1,250 for the first category and only 761 for the second. This difference can clearly be seen in the number of males and females per village as well. In the second classification, with average number of males and females being relatively larger in villages along the main route than in those that are not, the average population per village turns out to be 1,499 for the former and 883 for the latter. Moreover, as can be seen in Table 3.6, the number of both males and females is also higher in villages within 15 km of nearest AWR than in villages farther than 15 km from AWR. As such, the average number of persons living in villages within 15 km (798) is higher than in villages outside 15 km (719). The fourth classification shows that the average number of males and females in villages with road network greater than 7.5 km is significantly higher than those below it. The average population per village is 1383 for the high road network villages and 759 for villages with lower road network.

Table 3.5: Classifications I and II: Basic Population Characteristics

Figures in Average Unless Specified Otherwise

Sl. No.	Characteristics	Classification I		Classification II		Total
		Connected with AWR	Not Connected with AWR	Along Main Route	Outside Main Route	
1	Population	1250	761	1499	883	1016
	Males	638	392	766	453	521
	Females	611	369	733	430	496
2	Sex Ratio	952	944	952	947	952
3	Population below 6 years	210	149	241	164	181
	Males	107	76	122	83	92
	Females	103	73	119	80	89
4	Child - Population Ratio (%)	17.13	19.40	16.28	18.75	18.22
5	Child Sex Ratio	995	996	1008	992	966
6	Number of households	255	150	313	175	205
7	Family Size	4.90	5.06	4.75	5.04	4.97
8	Literacy Rate (percentage)	72.98	64.85	77.16	66.87	69.10
	Male	75.68	69.09	78.95	70.76	72.53
	Female	70.08	60.31	75.27	62.69	65.41
9	Population Density (per sq. km)	94	34	55	68	65

Source: Census, 2011

Table 3.6: Classifications III and IV: Basic Population Characteristics

Figures in Average Unless Specified Otherwise

Sl. No.	Characteristics	AWR	Classification III		Classification IV		Total
			Within 15 km	Outside 15 km	Below 7.5 km	Above 7.5 km	
1	Population	1250	798	719	759	1383	1016
	Males	638	411	369	391	706	521
	Females	611	386	350	369	677	496
2	Sex Ratio	952	937	951	942	956	948
3	Population below 6 years	210	157	140	144	233	181
	Males	107	80	71	74	118	92
	Females	103	77	69	70	115	89
4	Child - Population Ratio (%)	17.13	19.33	19.49	19.12	16.93	18.22
5	Child Sex Ratio	995	989	1004	986	1008	995
6	Number of households	255	157	141	150	282	205
7	Family Size	4.90	5.05	5.07	5.05	4.87	4.97
8	Literacy Rate (percentage)	72.98	63.71	66.15	64.49	75.67	69.10
	Male	75.68	68.41	69.87	68.86	77.77	72.53
	Female	70.08	58.67	62.18	59.77	73.46	65.41
9	Population Density (per sq. km)	94	40	26	86	34	65

Source: Census, 2011

The above analysis of total population shows that the average number of people residing in villages with better road connectivity is higher than the average for villages with poor road connectivity. On one hand, it can be hypothesised that people tend to reside in areas where there is better road connectivity as it brings with it numerous amenities. On the other hand, it may mean that provision of infrastructure is greatly influenced by the quantity of population considering the fact, among other factors, that the study area is a democratic state. At the same time, it is important to note that the areas where population is high are usually common service centres in which various facilities are available thus making the road network higher. In addition, villages with better road connectivity are usually engaged in settled cultivation more than others which make density of road higher through agricultural link roads and the like.

The second argument is sex ratio, defined here as the number of females per 1000 males in the population. It is an important social indicator to measure the extent of prevailing equity between males and females in a society at a given point of time. It is also often supposed that higher the human sex ratio, the higher is the development of that economy (South and Trent, 1988). Moreover, this type of study could be found in the works of Aggarwal (2013) and Ryhal and Punam (2009).

Table 3.5 and Table 3.6 shows that sex ratio is higher in villages connected with AWR at 952 while it is 944 for the unconnected villages. Moreover, for every 1000 males, there are 952 females in villages along the main route, while the average is 947 for those lying outside the route. However, the sex ratio is 937 for villages within 15 km which is lower than in villages farther than 15 km from AWR at 951. Lastly, the number of females per 1000 males is 956 and 942 for villages with road network above and below 7.5 km respectively. This denotes that the sex ratio is higher in villages with better road connectivity except for the third classification i.e., distance from AWR. Nevertheless, it may be concluded that road connectivity does have an effect on the sex ratio of the population since it was found to be higher in most of the classifications.

Next is the child population of the age group of 0-6 years which allows us to broadly analyse possible linkages with growth of population, particularly providing leads on fertility (Census of India, 2011).

For villages connected with AWR, the average number of children below six years is 210 while the same is 149 for unconnected ones. However, in terms of its ratio to total population, those not connected with AWR have a higher percentage at 19.40 while it is 17.13 per cent for connected villages. At the same time, the number of children below six years is 241 for villages along the main route and 164 outside main route. Here also, the number of males and females is significantly higher in the former than in the latter. A similar scenario like that of the first classification can be seen in the child ratio to population as the ratio is higher in villages outside main transport routes (18.75 per cent for outside main route; 16.28 per cent for along main route). For the third classification, the average number of children below the age of six is 157 for those within 15 km of the nearest AWR while it is 140 outside this area, with respective Child-Total Population Ratio of 19.33 per cent and 19.49 per cent. The road network classification also shows similar character as the number is significantly higher in villages above 7.5 km (233) than those below it (144). The child ratio to total population is 19.12 per cent for 'below 7.5 km' which is higher than the ratio for 'above 7.5 km' with 16.93 per cent.

Thus, it may be noted that in most cases, there are more children in villages with better road connectivity. This is in line with the analysis of total population where the number of people is higher in these areas. However, a distinct feature that came to light is the ratio of children to the total population being higher in villages with poor road connectivity, which may be translated as higher dependency ratio in these villages. In other words, in villages with poor road connectivity, there are more people, particularly children in this case, who are dependent on others.

Sex ratio (females per 1000 males) for the population of 0-6 years is the most important sex ratio because an adverse sex ratio would mean that fewer girls are being born compared to boys, thereby indicating discrimination against the female foetus (MacPherson, 2007). Although the state of Mizoram prides itself of no such discrimination, it is still a point of interest to check whether there are any differences between the various categories because of the importance attributed to it especially at the national level.

It can be seen from the same tables (Table 3.5 and 3.6) that the child sex ratio (females per 100 males) for connected villages (995) is slightly lower than for those not connected (966). In contrast, it is higher in villages along main route at 1008 while it is 992 in villages outside the main transport route. The averages for the third classification are 989 and 1004 for those within and farther than 15 km from AWR, while the child sex ratios are 986 and 1008 respectively for those 'below' and 'above' 7.5 km. These observations show that although the differences are not greatly significant, the child sex ratio is indeed higher for villages with better road connectivity.

The study also accounted the number of households from which average family size is derived. For the classification of AWR-connection, the average number of households for connected villages is 255 while it is only 150 for the unconnected ones. This incident is in line with the average number of persons residing in the areas. On the other hand, the average family size is higher in the latter than the former at 5.06 and 4.90, respectively. For the second classification, the average number of households is higher along the main transport route at 313, while it is 175 for those outside the transport route. The average family size, however, is 4.75 for along main route and 5.04 for outside main route which means that there are more persons living under one roof in the villages outside of the main transport route. It is also shown in the third classification that the number of households descends as we go farther from AWR availability, as their averages are 255, 157 and 141 for villages with AWR, within 15 km and outside 15 km of AWR, respectively. Alternately, it ascends in family size with average of 4.90, 5.05, and 5.07 persons per family. Furthermore, it can be seen that the average number of households in villages with road network above 7.5 km is 282 which is higher than the number of households per village with road network below 7.5 km whose average is 150. The average family size, however, is larger in 'below 7.5 km' (5.05) than in the 'above 7.5 km' (4.87) category.

The above examination shows that the average number of households is higher in villages with better road connectivity. This, again, is in consonance with the total number of population given in the earlier analysis. It also shows that the average family size is smaller in these villages than in villages with poor road connectivity. This may translate into better social and economic life in villages with better road connectivity as households with small family sizes would be able to educate their children well, provide better medical care as well as give them better housing and welfare services (Arthur, 2005).

The next characteristic taken under study is the literacy level. This is a vital indicator of development in a society as it greatly contributes to improving quality of life, particularly with regard to life expectancy, infant mortality, learning levels, and nutritional levels of children (Shah, 2013). Moreover, it may be added that literacy level and educational attainment are key variables in the Physical Quality of Life Index (PQLI) of Overseas Development Council and United Nations Development Programme's Human Development Index (HDI). As such, literacy rate of the people is considered an important variable in the study.

In the classification of whether or not the village is connected with AWR, literates occupy 72.98 per cent of the total population in the connected villages and 64.85 per cent in unconnected villages. Moreover, the male literacy rate for the first category is 75.68 per cent while the same is 69.09 per cent for the second. Female literacy rate is also higher in AWR-connected villages as 70.08 per cent are literates while for the unconnected, the average percentage is 60.31. Literacy rate with respect to the second classification also shows a higher number of literates in villages along the main transport route than those outside the main transport route. The percentages are 77.16 and 66.87 respectively. It is also higher for both the sexes in villages along the main route (78.95 for males; 75.27 for females) than in villages outside the main route (70.76 for males; 62.69 for females). In the third classification, it can be observed that the percentage of literates is slightly lower in villages within 15 km (63.71 per cent) than in villages outside 15 km (66.15 per cent) though both are lower than the literacy rate of AWR-connected villages. Moreover, the male literacy rate for villages within 15 km is 68.41 per cent which is lower than for villages outside 15 km of AWR at 69.87 per cent. Also, in villages within 15 km, the female literacy rate is 58.67 per cent which is again lower than the percentage for villages 15 km away from the nearest AWR at 62.18 per cent. The fourth classification shows that both male and female literacy rates are higher in villages with higher road network. In percentages, the literacy rates of males and females in villages with road network above 7.5 km are respectively 77.77 and 73.46 while the same are 68.86 and 59.77, respectively for males and females in villages with road network below 7.5 km. As such, the overall literacy rate for villages above 7.5 km is 75.67 per cent while it is 64.49 per cent for those below 7.5 km. Thus, in most of the classifications, the overall literacy rate and male and females rates are significantly higher in villages with better road connectivity. Since higher level of literacy leads to greater awareness and help people in acquiring new skills, it may be concluded that road connectivity does have a favourable impact on economic development.

Next is population density. Population density is simply the average number of people per square kilometre and is a way of measuring population distribution. It can be seen that the density of population per square kilometre is significantly higher in connected villages at 94 while it is only 34 for villages not connected with AWR. It is, however, higher in villages outside the main route with an average of 68 persons per square kilometre while the same is 55 for those along the state's main transport route. At the same time, population density was found to be higher in villages within 15 km of AWR with the average being 40 persons; while it is 26 persons per sq km for villages outside 15 km. However, it is higher in the villages with road network below 7.5 km at 86 persons per sq. km than in villages above 7.5 km road network which has an average number of 34 persons per sq km.

The above analysis of population density provided mixed results. While it is higher in the AWR-connected villages (Classification I) and in villages within 15 km (Classification III), the density of population is lower in villages along the main road (Classification II) and villages with road network above 7.5 km (Classification IV). However, it may also be stated that while high population density has been commonly portrayed as the main spanner in economic development, the 2011 World Population data showed that many nations with higher population density fare better on development counts.

Composition of Workers

Another approach in which the growth and development level of an area can be studied is through its employment status. Full, productive, and decent employment is the most important source of income security as it paves the way for broader social and economic advancement, strengthening individuals, their families and communities (United Nations, 2012). Studies of the impact of road connectivity on employment level can be seen in the works of Parida (2014), Mohapatra and Chandrasekhar (2007) and in other impact assessments of schemes promoting rural road connectivity undertaken by various agencies. As such, it is interesting to present workers' detail of the study areas and use it to check whether there are divergences in the economic activities of the population across the four connectivity classifications.

Table 3.7 shows the different ratios in our first (connectivity status) and second (main transport route) classifications and Table 3.8 presents the data with respect to their distance from the nearest AWR and in terms of road network.

Table 3.7 shows that the number of workers relative to their respective total population is higher in villages with better road connectivity. Elaborately, the ratio of total workers to total population in villages with AWR is 49.64 per cent while it is 48.48 per cent in the case of villages without AWR, which means that the working population is higher in the former than in the latter. It can also be seen in the second classification that there are more workers in the villages along the main route than in those outside the main transport route as 51.19 per cent in villages along the main route are workers while the same is 48.50 per cent for villages outside main route. Table 3.8 shows that the number of workers is higher in the villages nearer to the AWR as 48.85 per cent of the population in villages within 15 km of the nearest AWR are workers while it is 48.05 per cent for villages farther than 15 km. The fourth classification also shows higher work participation in the villages with higher road network. This is evident because the percentage of total workers to total population for villages with road network of more than 7.5 km is 50.95 per cent, while for villages below the same measure it is 47.78 per cent. Therefore, the above analysis showing the number of workers being higher in villages with better road connectivity may be translated as higher development level since employment is the source of income and a powerful tool of development through removal of poverty.

Moreover, the ratio of males to total workers in Classification I is 59.22 per cent for the AWR-connected villages while the same is 58.88 per cent for unconnected villages. The connected villages have a lower ratio of female workers to total workers (40.78 per cent) than the unconnected ones (41.12 per cent). This means that there are more female workers in villages not connected with AWR

Table 3.7: Classifications I and II: Population by Economic Activity

Figures in Average Unless Specified Otherwise

Sl. No.	Activity	Classification I		Classification II		Total
		Connected with AWR	Not Connected with AWR	Along Main Route	Outside Main Route	
1	Total Workers (%)	49.64	48.48	51.19	48.50	49.09
	Males	59.22	58.88	58.69	59.15	59.05
	Females	40.78	41.12	41.31	40.85	40.95
	Workers' Sex Ratio	725	747	727	738	735
2	Main Workers (%)	89.13	85.60	88.38	87.18	87.44
	Males	63.40	65.51	62.88	64.83	64.41
	Females	36.60	34.49	37.12	35.17	35.59
	Cultivators	68.46	72.79	62.81	72.66	4.58
	Agricultural Labourers	6.28	2.73	9.30	3.28	0.51
	Household Industry Workers	0.55	0.47	0.63	0.48	6.49
3	Marginal Workers (%)	5.83	7.21	6.20	6.57	30.89
	Males	31.37	30.37	31.60	30.69	54.60
	Females	57.15	51.81	60.36	53.01	46.68
	Cultivators	44.58	48.97	42.58	47.81	2.91
	Agricultural Labourers	18.34	8.24	23.93	10.64	13.52
	Household Industry Workers	3.07	2.74	3.71	2.69	2.91

Source: Census, 2011

Table 3.8: Classifications III and IV: Population by Economic Activity

Figures in Average Unless Specified Otherwise

Sl. No.	Activity	AWR	Classification III Within 15 km	Classification III Outside 15 km	Classification IV Below 7.5 km	Classification IV Above 7.5 km	Total
1	Total Workers (%)	49.64	48.85	48.05	47.78	50.95	49.09
	Males	59.22	60.03	57.55	59.58	58.31	59.05
	Females	40.78	39.97	42.45	40.42	41.69	40.95
	Workers' Sex Ratio	725	721	776	729	745	735
2	Main Workers (%)	89.13	87.95	82.89	86.41	88.92	87.44
	Males	63.40	65.62	65.39	65.62	62.69	64.41
	Females	36.60	34.38	34.61	34.38	37.31	35.59
	Cultivators	68.46	75.22	70.00	70.80	70.14	4.58
	Agricultural Labourers	6.28	2.86	2.58	4.25	5.05	0.51
	Household Industry Workers	0.55	0.35	0.61	0.39	0.69	6.49
3	Marginal Workers (%)	5.83	6.25	8.31	6.77	6.08	30.89
	Males	31.37	29.65	31.20	31.72	29.71	54.60
	Females	57.15	49.90	54.01	51.50	59.02	46.68
	Cultivators	44.58	46.18	52.18	47.45	45.57	2.91
	Agricultural Labourers	18.34	8.27	8.21	11.53	16.35	13.52
	Household Industry Workers	3.07	2.22	3.33	2.35	3.72	2.91

Source: Census, 2011

when measured in relation to the total population of workers. In Classification II, the percentage of male workers to total workers is slightly lower in villages along transport route (58.69 per cent) than in villages outside the route (59.15 per cent). The ratio of female workers to total workers, on the other hand, is higher in villages along the main routes (41.31 per cent) than in the villages outside the main routes (40.85 per cent). This means that female work participation is higher in the villages along the main routes. For Classification III, the data show that the ratio of males to total workers is higher in villages within 15 km (60.03 per cent) than in villages outside 15 km of AWR (57.55 per cent). Females Total Workers Ratio, on the other hand, shows that in villages farther than 15 km, the ratio is 42.45 per cent, which is higher than the ratio for villages within 15 km at 39.97 per cent. It is also shown that the ratio of male workers to total workers is higher in villages with 'below 7.5 km' road network (59.58 per cent) than in villages with road network 'above 7.5 km' (58.31 per cent). On the other hand, percentage of female workers with respect to total workers is higher in villages with greater road network as the ratio is 41.69 per cent while the percentage of the same is 40.42 for villages with lower road network. This confirms that female work participation is higher in villages having greater network of roads.

The above analysis of the percentage of male workers to total workers shows mixed results. While the ratio is higher in villages along the main route (Classification II) and those within 15 km of AWR (Classification III) than their respective counterparts, it is lower in villages connected with AWR (Classification I) and those with road network above 7.5 km (Classification IV). The opposite is evidently true for the female ratio to total workers in the classifications. Therefore, the study cannot give a clear-cut conclusion about the male and female percentages of total workers. This would obviously result in the same effect on the workers' sex ratio.

In Table 3.7, the workers' sex ratio (females per 1000 males) is higher in unconnected villages than in villages connected with AWR as their averages per village are 747 and 725 females per 1000 males, respectively. Also, the ratio is higher in villages lying outside of the main transport route at 738 while it is 727 for villages along the main route. Table 3.8 shows that female workers per 1000 male workers is highest in villages that are farther than 15 km from AWR (776) followed by AWR-connected villages (725) while villages within 15 km has the lowest ratio (721). Moreover, the ratio for villages with road network above 7.5 km is 745 females per 1000 males which is higher than its counterpart i.e., below 7.5 km whose ratio is 729. Therefore, it may be stated that an AWR connection and distance from it may not translate into higher sex ratio of workers, but if the focus is on such, then the village has to have daily transport facilities connecting it with other villages and also a high network of roads.

The population of total workers was further broken down into 'main workers' and 'marginal workers'. It is important to add here that the Census of India defines main workers as workers who had worked for the major part of the reference period (i.e. 6 months or more) while marginal workers are those workers who had worked for less than six months during the reference period.

The number of main workers was found to be higher in villages with better road connectivity as its percentage to total workers is higher in all the classifications. It can be seen from the table that the ratio of main workers to total workers for AWR-connected villages is 89.13 per cent, which is higher than its counterpart at 85.60 per cent. This ratio is also higher for the case of 'along main road' at 88.38 per cent while it is 87.18 per cent for 'outside main road' in the second classification. It can also be seen that among the total number of workers, there are more workers who fall into the 'main workers' category in villages within 15 km as the ratio is 87.95 per cent while it is 82.89 per cent for villages farther than 15 km. There are also larger numbers of main workers in villages with higher road network as the ratio is higher in villages with road network above 7.5 km (88.92 per cent) than in villages with road network below 7.5 km (86.41 per cent).

It can also be deduced from Table 3.7 that the number of main workers who are males is higher in villages not connected with AWR as their percentages are 65.51 and 63.40 per cent respectively. On the other hand, the share of females in main workers is higher in villages with AWR at 36.60 per cent while it is 34.49 per cent in villages without AWR. This means that the number of female workers categorised as main workers is higher in AWR-connected villages. It is also shown that the male population who are main workers is higher in villages outside the main route at 64.83 per cent while the same is 62.88 per cent in villages along the main transport route. The data for the female population, however, shows that the percentage of female main workers is higher in villages along the main route at 37.12 per cent than in villages outside the main route at 35.17 per cent. Through Table 3.8, it may be noted that the ratio of males to the number of main workers is slightly higher in villages within 15 km of AWR than in villages outside 15 km. Their shares are 65.62 and 65.39 per cent, respectively. At the same time, the number of females is higher in villages outside 15 km (34.61 per cent) than in villages within 15 km (34.38 per cent). It is also shown that for villages below 7.5 km of road network, the percentage of males among main workers is 65.62 per cent which is higher than the percentage for villages above 7.5 km at 62.69 per cent. The opposite is true for the female population. 37.31 per cent of the main workers in villages with road network above 7.5 km, are female workers, while for villages with road network below 7.5 km, it is 34.38 per cent. This denotes that, in respect of the total main workers, there are more female workers in villages with higher road network.

Consequently, what can be derived from the particular examination is – the percentage of male main workers is higher in villages lying outside the main route and within 15 km of AWR while they are lower in villages connected with AWR and in villages that possess above 7.5 km road network than their respective adversaries. However, in most of the cases, the percentage of female main workers among total main workers was found to be higher in villages with better road connectivity.

The ratio of cultivators to the total main workers was also analysed. In its simplest form, a cultivator is a person engaged in cultivation of land owned or held and has effective supervision or direction in cultivation. The analysis shows that the percentage of cultivators is higher for unconnected villages (72.79 per cent) than the connected ones (68.46 per cent). This means that in relation of total main workers, the number of cultivators is higher in the unconnected villages than in the connected villages. It is also higher in villages outside of the main route at 72.66 per cent while for villages along main route, it is 62.81 per cent. Moreover, computation of the ratio with respect to distance from AWR shows that it is higher in villages within 15 km than in villages outside 15 km of AWR as their percentages are respectively 75.22 and 70. On the other hand, the average is higher in villages below 7.5 km road network at 70.80 per cent, while it is 70.14 per cent for villages above 7.5 km. Thus, in most cases, the percentage share of cultivators in the total main workers is higher in villages with poor road connectivity.

It was also an interest to check the percentage of agricultural labourers. An agricultural labourer may be defined as a person who works on another person's land for wages in money or kind or share. The analysis shows that the ratio of agricultural labourers in relation to the total number of main workers is higher in AWR-connected villages as the ratio of the same is 6.28 per cent while it is 2.73 per cent for unconnected villages. It can also be seen that the percentage is higher in villages along the main route as the ratio of main agricultural labourers to main workers is significantly higher at 9.30 per cent while the same is only 3.28 per cent for villages outside the main route. At the same time, it is also higher in villages within 15 km as their ratio to the total number of main workers is 2.86 per cent while the same is 2.58 per cent for villages farther than 15 km from the nearest AWR. The road network classification also shows that the ratio is higher in villages above 7.5 km road network at 5.05 per cent while it is 4.25 per cent for villages below 7.5 km. It can be consequently stated that the number of agricultural labourers, i.e., persons working on other people's land for wages is higher in villages with better road connectivity.

It was also found that there are more household industry workers in villages with better road connectivity than in villages with relatively inferior connectivity. From the tables, it can be derived that the average of household industry workers as a ratio of main workers is 0.55 per cent for AWR-connected villages which is higher than its counterpart at 0.47 per cent. The same can be observed in the second classification as the ratio for villages along transport route is 0.63 per cent which is higher than the percentage for villages outside transport route at 0.48 per cent. However, villages lying farther than 15 km from the nearest AWR have higher number of industrial main workers. While it is 0.61 per cent for this category, the percentage for villages within 15 km of AWR is 0.35. The ratio for villages with higher road network above 7.5 km is 0.69 per cent which is significantly greater than the ratio for villages with lower road network at 0.39 per cent.

The case of marginal workers was also taken into account in the study. As already stated, marginal workers are workers who worked for less than six months within a reference year. The ratio of marginal workers to total workers is lower in villages connected with AWR at 5.83 per cent while it is 7.21 per cent for villages not connected with AWR. The same is higher in the case of villages outside the main route as its ratio is 6.57 per cent while it is 6.20 per cent for villages lying along the main route. This percentage of marginal workers out of total workers is also higher in villages outside 15 km of AWR at 8.31 while the same is 6.25 per cent for villages within 15 km. The percentage for villages where road network is below 7.5 km is higher than its counterpart as the share of marginal workers to total workers is 6.77 per cent for villages with lower road network and 6.08 per cent for villages with higher road network. Thus, it can be seen that the percentage of marginal workers is higher in villages with poor road connectivity. In other words, out of the total workers in the village, there are more marginal workers in villages with poor road connectivity than in villages with better road connectivity.

In spite of the fact that the percentage of marginal workers is lower in villages with AWR connection, the ratio of male marginal workers to total marginal workers for connected villages is 31.37 per cent, which is higher than 30.37 per cent for unconnected villages. The ratio of female workers to marginal workers is 57.15 per cent for connected villages and 51.81 per cent for unconnected villages. Classification II shows that the percentage is higher in both the sexes in villages along the main route although the percentage of the female marginal workers (60.36 per cent for 'along main route' and 53.01 per cent for 'outside main route') is more significant in both the cases than their male counterpart (31.60 per cent for 'along main route' and 30.69 per cent for 'outside main route').

In contrast, percentage of males and females among total marginal workers shows that the percentages for villages farther from AWR are higher (31.20 per cent for males, 54.01 per cent for females) than those for villages nearer to AWR (29.65 per cent for males, 49.90 per cent for females). This implies that the number of marginal workers becomes higher as we go farther from AWR. Lastly, in the classification of villages by their road network, the number of male workers is higher in villages of lesser road network than in villages with road network above 7.5 km as the ratios show 31.72 per cent and 29.71 per cent, respectively. On the other hand, the percentage for female workers is higher in the 'below 7.5 km' category at 59.02 per cent while it is 51.50 per cent for 'above 7.5 km'. As such, a clear-cut conclusion regarding male marginal workers cannot be derived from the above interpretation as it shows mixed results across the four classifications. However, it may be noted that in most cases, the participation of the female population is higher in villages with better road connectivity than in villages with poor road connectivity.

Like that of main cultivators, there are more marginal cultivators in villages with poor road connectivity when the same is taken as a percentage of total marginal workers. Here, the average number of marginal cultivators is higher in the case of villages not connected with AWR as its percentage to marginal workers is 48.97 per cent while the same is 44.58 per cent for villages connected with AWR. Also, the percentage of marginal cultivators to total marginal ratio is higher at 47.81 per cent for villages outside the main route and 42.58 per cent for villages along the main route. Moreover, the percentage is higher in villages outside 15 km of AWR as it is 52.18 per cent in these villages while in villages within 15 km, it is 46.18 per cent. The table also shows that the percentage is higher in villages with road network below 7.5 km at 47.45 per cent while the same is 45.57 per cent for villages with road network above 7.5 km.

Again in Table 3.7, it is shown that the percentage of marginal agricultural labourers to marginal workers is significantly higher in the connected villages at 18.34 per cent while the same is only 8.24 per cent for unconnected villages. The percentage of the same is also higher in villages along the main route (23.93 per cent) than in villages outside the main route (10.64 per cent). Table 3.8 shows that the percentage of agricultural labourers is higher in villages within 15 km at 8.27 per cent than in villages farther than 15 km from AWR whose share in total marginal workers is 8.21 per cent. Moreover, it is higher in villages with greater road network at 16.35 per cent while for villages with lower road network, it is 11.53 per cent. Thus, like that of main agricultural labourers, the ratio of agricultural labourers who are marginal workers is higher in villages with better road connectivity.

The data for the ratio of household industry workers to total marginal workers shows that AWR-connected villages have a higher percentage at 3.07 per cent while the same is 2.74 per cent for villages not connected with AWR. At the same time, it is also higher in villages along the main transport route at 3.71 per cent than in villages outside the route whose share amounts to 2.69 per cent. It can also be seen that the percentage is the highest in villages that are more than 15 km away from the nearest AWR with 3.33 per cent while in villages nearer to AWR, the percentage is 2.22. However, it can be also be seen that villages with road network greater than 7.5 km have a higher percentage at 3.72 per cent while for its counterpart, villages with road network under 7.5 km, it is at 2.35 per cent. Therefore, except for the 'distance from AWR' classification, it can be seen that there are more industrial workers in villages with better road connectivity than in villages with inferior road connectivity.

The entire analysis of the population according to their economic activities can be summarised in the following notable points:

First, total workers' ratio is higher in villages with better road connectivity. A reasonable assumption may be the availability of more livelihood options and the possibility of shifting from agriculture to service sector in these villages. At the same time, the percentage is low in villages with poor road connectivity probably because of the high child ratio to population in these villages which consequently translates into high dependency ratio.

Second, even though the total workers' ratio is lower in villages with poor road connectivity, a notable feature is the contribution of female workers. The reason for this situation may be the extensive practice of shifting cultivation in these areas. In a traditional set up, male and female work forces have equal contribution in jhumming cultivation in most of the cases and as such, female work participation was found to be high in these villages.

Third, there are more marginal workers in villages with poor road connectivity. The definition of 'marginal workers' as given in Census of India as those who worked for less than six months would support the assumed reason for this feature of high marginal workers to being a result of the seasonal nature of the state's agriculture, jhumming to be exact. On the other hand, a distinctive trait found in the analysis of marginal workers is that while the overall percentage is higher in poorly connected villages, the female marginal workers' percentage is higher in villages with better road connectivity.

Fourth, the percentage of industrial workers is higher in villages with better road connectivity. At the same time, there is a higher percentage of agricultural labourers in these villages as well. It may be hypothesised that the problem of land availability has emerged as a result of road connectivity, especially in the areas along the main transport route. The lands in the villages with better road connectivity attract wealthy investors (Golmohammadi, 2012). At the same time, the price of such lands rises up (Chambers, 2006). So, the workers are required to work in other people's farms and become agricultural labourers. Meanwhile, with the development of communication, households belonging to villages with better road connectivity may have a better chance of adopting industrial livelihood occupations like trade and transport services, among others, thus resulting in the higher percentage of household industry workers in these villages.

Land Use Pattern

Having major impacts not only on the livelihood of rural population but also on natural resources, proper land use practices have been rightly viewed to have effects on the economy and environment. As the main occupation of the people in developing countries is agriculture and with the growing attention towards sustainable development, land use is an integral part of development processes that cannot be viewed in isolation from other critical elements of that process, namely social and economic planning (Thomas, 2001). Different literatures regarding the relationship between road connectivity and land use can be found in the works of Huang and Hsieh (2014), Freitas et al. (2009), and Alba and Beimborn (2004). Therefore, it is an academic interest to study the land use patterns of the areas using the same set of classifications.

Here, the cases considered are percentage area of wet rice cultivation, agriculture plantation, forest cover, and jhum size per household. In addition to these, the total area of the villages is presented as well. Table 3.9 and 3.10 shows the land use data with respect to the four classifications.

Like the former analyses, Classification I is based on whether the village is connected with AWR or not and Classification II on whether they are along the main transport route of the state. These are given in Table 3.9. At the same time, Table 3.10 shows Classification III, in which the land use data is analysed according to the distance of villages from the nearest AWR, and Classification IV, which is based on the road network in the village.

The area of wet rice cultivation (WRC) to village area is higher in the AWR-connected villages with the percentage being 0.85 per cent while it is 0.83 per cent for villages not connected with AWR. In the second classification, it can be seen that the percentage of WRC area is higher for villages outside main road (0.89 per cent) than for villages along main road (0.69 per cent). At the same time, the percentage of WRC area is higher in villages nearer to AWR than those far from it. For villages within 15 km, it is 1.05 per cent while it is 0.58 per cent for those outside 15 km of AWR. However, the percentage of land under WRC is larger in villages with lower road network. Their percentages are 1.01 and 0.60 for villages below and above 7.5 km respectively. Thus, the data present mixed results where the percentage of WRC area is higher in villages connected with AWR and in villages within 15 km of the nearest AWR than their respective opponents while it is higher in villages outside main route and villages with road network below 7.5 km.

Table 3.9: Classifications I and II: Land Use Data

Figures in Average Unless Specified Otherwise

Sl. No.	Cases	Classification I		Classification II		Total
		Connected with AWR	Not Connected with AWR	Along Main Route	Outside Main Route	
1	WRC Area (%)	0.85	0.83	0.69	0.89	0.84
2	Agriculture Plantation Area (%)	0.31	0.09	0.45	0.14	0.20
3	Forest Area (%)	73.88	76.27	75.57	74.88	75.03
4	Jhum Size per Household (Hectare)	3.44	4.36	2.81	4.17	3.88
5	Average Area of the Village (sq km)	37.86	36.43	40.34	36.30	37.18
6	Area within 1km from motorable road (sq km)	11.73	2.98	14.17	5.72	7.55

Source: Mizoram Remote Sensing Application Centre, 2014

Table 3.10: Classifications III and IV: Land Use Data

Figures in Average Unless Specified Otherwise

Sl. No.	Cases		Classification III		Classification IV		
		AWR	Within 15 km	Outside 15 km	Below 7.5 km	Above 7.5 km	Total
1	WRC Area (%)	0.85	1.05	0.58	1.01	0.60	0.84
2	Agriculture Plantation Area (%)	0.31	0.08	0.10	0.11	0.34	0.20
3	Forest Area (%)	73.88	75.19	77.52	74.75	75.42	75.03
4	Jhum Size per Household (Hectare)	3.44	4.27	4.45	3.85	3.91	3.88
5	Average Area of the Village (sq km)	37.86	33.37	39.94	30.65	46.50	37.18
6	Area within 1km from motorable road (sq km)	11.73	4.03	1.79	1.31	16.46	7.55

Source: Mizoram Remote Sensing Application Centre, 2014

In the case of agriculture plantation area, there is a significant difference between villages connected with AWR and those that are not, the percentage being 0.31 for the former and only 0.09 per cent for the latter. Moreover, it can be seen that plantation is being undertaken more extensively in villages lying along the main transport route as the percentage of agriculture plantation area is higher in these villages at 0.45 per cent while it is 0.14 per cent for villages outside the main route. The percentage, however, is higher in villages farther than 15 km as it is 0.10 per cent while it is 0.08 per cent for villages within 15 km. At the same time, agriculture plantation area is greater in villages with higher road network at 0.34 per cent for villages with road network above 7.5 km and 0.11 per cent for those below it. Consequently, what can be seen is that in most of the cases, agriculture plantation area is higher in villages with better road connectivity than in villages with poor road connectivity.

Percentage of forest cover area to average village area is higher in villages not connected with AWR as it stands at 76.27 per cent while it is 73.88 per cent for the connected ones. However, the percentage is higher in villages along the main transport route at 75.57 per cent while the same is 74.88 per cent for villages outside the main route. It can also be observed that percentage of forest cover area becomes denser as we move farther away from AWR. It is 73.88 per cent, 75.19 per cent, and 77.52 per cent for villages with AWR, within 15 km, and outside 15 km of AWR, respectively. At the same time, the percentage area of villages under forest cover is slightly higher in villages with road network above 7.5 km with 75.42 per cent while it is 74.75 per cent for villages below 7.5 km road network. Therefore, the data for percentage of forest cover area in village area show that it is lower in villages with AWR connection and in villages within 15 km of AWR, while it is slightly higher both in villages along main route and villages with road network above 7.5 km.

The average jhum area per household was found to be higher in villages not connected with AWR at 4.36 hectares while the same is 3.44 hectares for AWR-connected villages. Moreover, it is higher in villages outside the main transport route at 4.17 hectares than in villages along the route with an average percentage of 2.81. The percentage is higher in villages farther than 15 km from AWR (4.45 hectares) than in villages within 15 km (4.27 hectares). On the other hand, the average area under jhum cultivation for a household is higher in villages with greater road network at 3.91 hectares while its counterpart is at 3.85 hectares. It should however be noted that the area of jhum cover for the study areas as a whole turned out to be 3.88 hectares per household per village which is larger than anticipated. The reason may be because of the fact that the data was derived through geographic information system which included both the current jhum and current fallow areas. However, the current fallow is considered here as operational holding if the entire area of operational holding is under current fallow during the reference year but was cultivated in the preceding year.

The average area of villages is slightly higher in the case of AWR-connected villages at 37.86 sq. km, while for the unconnected ones, it is 36.43 sq. km. At the same time, it is larger for villages along main route as the average for it is 40.34 sq. km while it is 36.30 for villages outside the main route. This average village area, however, shows a contrasting feature in the third classification as it is the lowest in villages within 15 km of the nearest AWR (33.37 sq. km) while it is the highest in villages with a distance of more than 15 km from AWR (39.94 sq. km). On the other hand, villages with higher road network have larger area (46.50 sq. km) than villages with low road network (30.65 sq. km). Therefore, the area of the village in most of the classifications is larger in villages with better road connectivity.

The area of the village within 1 km from the motorable road (National Highway, State Highway, District Road, and Village Road) is significantly higher in AWR-connected area as the average turned out to be 11.73 sq. km while the same is 2.98 sq. km for the villages without AWR. Moreover, for villages along the main transport route, the average is 14.17 sq. km which is significantly higher than its counterpart whose average area is 5.72 sq. km. This measure is higher in villages within 15 km of AWR (4.03 sq. km) than in villages outside 15 km of AWR (1.79 sq. km). However, it should be noted that both these averages are well below the state average. Lastly, villages with higher road network have a significantly higher area of their village within 1 km from motorable road as the average for these villages is 16.64 sq. km while for villages with lower road network, the average is 1.31 sq. km. It can thus be concluded that the villages with better road connectivity unsurprisingly have more area of their village within 1 km from motorable road.

Some of the notable observations of the analysis of the various cases of land use are given in the following:

First, the percentage of WRC area to total village area is higher in villages connected with AWR and in villages that are within 15 km of the nearest AWR. However, it is lower in villages with high road network and those along the main transport route than their respective adversaries. This is due to the fact that there are villages that are connected with AWR but do not lie along the main route having large tracts of land under WRC. The cases of Buhchangphai, Meidum, and Bukvannei villages of Kolasib districts may be cited. Possessing WRC areas of 22.69 per cent, 19.48 per cent and 14.72 per cent respectively, they are among the villages having the highest area under WRC in the whole study area. As such, the percentage is higher for villages outside the main route since these percentages shoot up the average percentage of the category.

Second, it can be stated that agricultural plantation area is highly correlated with road connectivity because the percentages for the villages with better road connectivity are significantly higher. Considering the topography of Mizoram, WRC might not be a possible option for the agricultural sector because the area for such cultivation would be limited by the state's terrain. An alternative practice to move the people away from the unsustainable practice of jhumming to sustainable cultivation would be agricultural plantation / settled cultivation like horticultural crops, rubber, etc. As such, the prevalence of agricultural plantation area may be viewed as one of the development indicators, especially for the agricultural sector. The percentage area being higher in villages with better road connectivity suggests that agriculture development is greater in these villages.

Third, percentage of forest cover area is higher in villages not connected with AWR and villages outside 15 km of nearest AWR than their counterparts while it is lower for villages with road network below 7.5 km and for villages outside the main route. This, again, may be due to the presence of high percentages in villages that are along the main route as a result of sanctuaries like Ngengpui Wildlife Sanctuary and Blue Mountain Sanctuary. The possibility of these sanctuaries raising the average percentage of forest area for these villages cannot be ruled out.

Fourth, the average jhum area per household per village is lower in villages with better road connectivity. In other words, the practice of jhumming is being undertaken more extensively in villages with poor road connectivity.

Lastly, in most cases, the average area of the village is larger in villages with better road connectivity. Moreover, the area of the village within 1 km from motorable land also shows a favourable situation for villages with better road connectivity. Therefore, it may be concluded that the village road network is influenced by its connectivity status while the reverse would also hold true to that effect.

Basic Social Infrastructures

Social infrastructures, like economic infrastructures, are deemed to possess enormous externalities in which social marginal productivity exceeds private marginal productivity (Kularatne, 2006) and as such, it is of interest to identify and analyse certain basic social infrastructures in order to know whether road connectivity has effect on the availability of these infrastructures which are crucial for creating sustainable communities. The social infrastructures identified for the study are educational facilities, amount of piped water supplied which is measured in litres per capita per day (LPCD), and the health care institutions and health care providers present in villages.

a) Educational Facilities

The study analysed the educational institutions present in the villages because education in every sense is one of the fundamental factors of development. Various studies have shown that well-educated societies have lower rates of violence and crime, and societies that emphasise accessible, effective education see their economies improve as well. Moreover, one of the indicators of educational development is the number of teachers available per student because a high teacher-student ratio (or low student-teacher ratio) can increase student achievement and provide lasting academic benefits by closing the achievement gap, promoting individualized achievement and encouraging greater participation in class. This test of the effect of road connectivity on the educational sector has been done at length by various authors like Golmohammadi (2012), Castaing (2011) and Umoren et al. (2009) who, among many others, have found a close relation between the status of road connectivity and education. Here in the present study, the number of schools, students, and teachers in each village were collected and are presented in averages in Table 3.11 and Table 3.12.

Starting from the total number of schools, it can be seen in Table 3.11 that the average number of schools in villages connected with AWR is 5.48 which is higher than in villages not connected with AWR whose average is 3.42. The ratio of teachers to students is also higher for the AWR-connected villages at 10.11 teachers per 100 students while it is 9.49 for the unconnected ones. Another conclusion that can be drawn from the table is that there are more schools in villages along main transport route than in villages outside the route. A significant difference between the two categories of villages can be observed as the average for the former is 6.54 while it is 3.93 for the latter. The teacher-student ratio is also higher in villages along the main transport route at 10.30 while the same is 9.68 for villages lying outside the main route of the state. In the third classification (shown in Table 3.12), the number of schools decreases as we move farther from AWR. As is shown, the average is 5.48 for villages with AWR while it is 3.45 for villages within 15 km of AWR and 3.39 for villages outside 15 km. The average number of teachers per 100 students, however, shows a different picture as it is the highest in 'AWR' (10.11), followed by 'Outside 15 km' (9.84) and then by 'Within 15 km' (9.17). In the 'Road Network' classification shown in the same table, it can be seen that villages with road network equal to or higher than 7.5 km has larger number of schools at 6.01 per village while it is only 3.44 for villages with road network lower than 7.5 km. Moreover, the teacher-student ratio is also higher in villages with road network 7.5 km or higher, as the average is 10.28 while the same is 9.48 in villages with road network lower than 7.5 km.

Table 3.11: Classifications I and II: Educational Institutions and Enrolment Details

Figures in Average Unless Specified Otherwise

Sl. No.	Details	Classification I		Classification II		Total
		Connected with AWR	Not Connected with AWR	Along Main Route	Outside Main Route	
1	No. of Primary Schools	2.71	1.76	3.19	2.00	2.26
	Teacher-Student Ratio (%)	6.42	5.76	6.52	5.99	6.11
2	No. of Middle Schools	1.88	1.27	2.26	1.40	1.59
	Teacher-Student Ratio (%)	14.24	14.32	14.12	14.32	14.28
3	No. of High Schools	0.80	0.38	0.96	0.49	0.59
	Teacher-Student Ratio (%)	12.10	7.02	13.25	8.69	9.68
4	No. of Higher Secondary Schools	0.10	0.01	0.13	0.03	0.06
	Teacher-Student Ratio (%)	1.30	0.06	1.84	0.40	0.71
5	Total No. of Schools (1+2+3+4)	5.48	3.42	6.54	3.93	4.50
	Teacher-Student Ratio (%)	10.11	9.49	10.30	9.68	9.81

Source: Field Survey, 2014

Table 3.12: Classifications III and IV: Educational Institutions and Enrolment Details

Figures in Average Unless Specified Otherwise

Sl. No.	Details	AWR	Classification III		Classification IV		Total
			Within 15 km	Outside 15 km	Below 7.5 km	Above 7.5 km	
1	No. of Primary Schools	2.71	1.70	1.83	1.75	2.99	2.26
	Teacher-Student Ratio (%)	6.42	5.57	5.99	5.94	6.34	6.11
2	No. of Middle Schools	1.88	1.33	1.20	1.26	2.07	1.59
	Teacher-Student Ratio (%)	14.24	14.19	14.46	13.78	14.99	14.28
3	No. of High Schools	0.80	0.39	0.36	0.42	0.84	0.59
	Teacher-Student Ratio (%)	12.10	7.14	6.89	7.63	12.59	9.68
4	No. of Higher Secondary Schools	0.10	0.02	0.01	0.01	0.12	0.06
	Teacher-Student Ratio (%)	1.30	0.04	0.09	0.08	1.61	0.71
5	Total No. of Schools (1+2+3+4)	5.48	3.45	3.39	3.44	6.01	4.50
	Teacher-Student Ratio (%)	10.11	9.17	9.84	9.48	10.28	9.81

Source: Field Survey, 2014

Therefore, the above analysis shows that the number of schools per village is higher in villages with better road connectivity than in villages with poor road connectivity. Moreover, the teacher-student ratio measured here as the number of teachers per 100 students is higher in most of the classifications of villages with better road connectivity. As such, it may be concluded that the existence of schools and availability of educators are related to the connectivity status of the rural areas.

The study also identified and analysed these educational facilities at the different standards – primary, middle, high, and higher secondary schools. This has been done to identify the standards in which there are significant differences between each category of the different classifications.

In the first classification, the number of primary schools is significantly higher in villages connected with AWR as its average is 2.71 while the same is 1.76 for villages not connected with AWR. The teacher-student ratio is also higher in the former case as the average number of teachers per 100 students in primary schools is 6.42 for the connected villages and 5.76 for the unconnected ones. The same can also be seen in the second classification as the average number of primary schools is 3.19 for villages along main transport route while it is 2.00 for the other villages. The teacher-student ratio is also higher in villages along the route (6.52) than in villages lying outside main transport route (5.99). At the same time, Table 3.12 shows that while the average number of primary schools is highest in villages with AWR, it is lowest in villages within 15 km of AWR at 1.70 and its counterpart is slightly higher at 1.83 primary schools per village. The same pattern can also be observed in the number of teachers per 100 students in primary schools, as the average for villages within 15 km of AWR is 5.57, which is lower than the average for villages farther than 15 km at 5.99. Again, they both are lower than the number of teachers in villages with AWR. The fourth classification shows that villages with road network above 7.5 km have more number of primary schools as the average for these villages is 2.99 while it is 1.75 for villages with lower road network. At the same time, the average number of primary school teachers per 100 students is 6.34 for villages having road network above 7.5 km while the same is 5.94 for villages with road network lower than 7.5 km. Therefore, the study of primary schools shows that in most of the classifications, there are more primary schools and more teachers per 100 students in villages with better road connectivity.

The average number of middle schools is higher in villages connected with AWR at 1.88 while the same is 1.27 in villages not connected with AWR. However, the average number of middle school teachers per 100 students is lower in the former (14.24) than in the latter (14.32). The classification of villages into 'along main route' and 'outside main route' also shows that the number of middle schools is higher in the former category than in the latter as their averages are respectively 2.26 and 1.40. The teacher-student ratio, however, is higher in villages outside the main route as the average is 14.32 while it is 14.12 for villages along the main route. It can also be seen from Table 3.12 that the number of middle schools is lower as we move farther from AWR. While the average for villages with AWR is 1.88, it is 1.33 and 1.20 for villages within 15 km and outside 15 km of AWR, respectively. On the other hand, the teacher per 100 student average is the highest in villages farther than 15 km from the nearest AWR (14.46) followed by villages with AWR (14.24) and villages within 15 km (14.19). The classification according to their network of road shows that villages with higher road network have a greater number of middle schools and teacher-student ratio. The average number of middle schools for villages with road network above 7.5 km is 2.07, which is higher than its counterpart at 1.26. At the same time, the average number of middle school teachers per 100 students is 14.99 for villages with higher road network while the same is 13.78 for villages with lower road network.

It can be seen from the above analysis that there are more middle schools in villages that possess better road connectivity. However, the teacher-student ratio of middle schools gives a mixed result. The number of teachers per 100 students of middle school standard is higher in villages with AWR and in villages with road network above 7.5 km while it is lower in villages along main route and those within 15 km of AWR. Therefore, it may be concluded that while the establishment of middle schools is related to their road connectivity status, the presence of teachers for middle school standard is not affected by the village being along the main transport route or its distance from AWR, but is affected by the village's road network and its AWR connectivity status.

The data for high school level of education shows that the average number of high schools in villages connected with AWR is 0.80 which is higher than the number for villages not connected with AWR whose average is 0.38. At the same time, the average number of high school teachers per 100 students in villages connected with AWR is 12.10, which is again higher than the average number of teachers per students in villages not connected with AWR at 7.02. The second classification also shows that more high schools are established in villages along the main route as the average for it is 0.96 while it is 0.49 per village for those lying outside the main transport route. In addition, the number of teachers per 100 students is higher along main route at 13.25 while for those outside the main route, the average is 8.69. It can also be seen that the average is higher in villages within 15 km (0.39) than in villages outside 15 km (0.36) of AWR. The teacher-student ratio for this classification is also higher in villages within 15 km as the average for it stands at 7.14 while for the outside 15 km category, it is 6.89 per village. Lastly, the number of high schools in villages with road network above 7.5 km is 0.84 per village which is higher than the average for villages below 7.5 km road network at 0.42. Moreover, the average number of teachers per 100 students is higher for villages that have road network above 7.5 km than for villages below 7.5 km road network. Their averages are 12.59 and 7.63, respectively. Thus, it may be stated that the establishment of high schools is related to the connectivity status as the averages of number of high schools and teachers per 100 students are higher in villages with better road connectivity.

Lastly, the average number of higher secondary schools for villages connected with AWR stands at 0.10 which is higher than the average for villages without AWR connection at only 0.01. The average teacher-student ratio is also higher in the former (1.30) than in the latter (0.06). At the same time, the average number of higher secondary schools is greater in villages along the main route at 0.13 than in villages outside the main route whose average is 0.03. The teacher-student ratio is also higher in the former at 1.84 while in the latter, it is 0.40. Classification according to the distance from AWR shows that the average number of higher secondary schools is slightly higher in villages within 15 km (0.02) than in villages outside 15 km (0.01). However, the teacher-student ratio for villages within 15 km is lower at 0.04 than for villages farther than 15 km, the ratio of which is 0.09. In addition, the number of higher secondary schools is higher in villages with road network above 7.5 km as the average for it is 0.12 while the same is 0.01 for villages with road network below 7.5 km. The teacher-student ratio is also higher in the former (1.61) than in the latter (0.08). Conclusively, it can be stated that the number of higher secondary schools available and teacher-pupil ratio is more favourable in villages with better road connectivity as their averages are higher for these villages in almost all the cases.

Therefore, the analysis of the number of schools present in each village and the number of teachers available for the total number of students shows that villages with better road connectivity enjoy better educational facilities. The average number of schools was found to be higher in villages with superior road connectivity than in villages with poor road connectivity in most of the cases. Moreover, the teacher-student ratio was also found to be higher in almost all the cases in favour of better connected villages. Therefore, it may be concluded that the promotion of education is taken up more extensively in villages that have a high level of road connectivity.

b) Drinking Water Supply

Another important component of social infrastructure is water supply and so, the study included the quantity of drinking water supply as one of the development

Table 3.13: Piped Water Supply

Figures in Average

Classification	Cases	Litres per Capita per Day
I Connectivity Status	Connected with AWR	33.79
	Not Connected with AWR	31.27
II Main Transport Route	Along Main Route	39.58
	Outside Main Route	30.51
III Distance from AWR	AWR	33.79
	Within 15 km	29.02
	Outside 15 km	33.86
IV Road Network	Below 7.5 km	31.05
	Above 7.5 km	34.77
	Total	32.58

Source: Public Health Engineering Dept, Mizoram 2015

variables. Though access to drinking water is not a major problem for the state, piped water supply is quite poor. Since unpolluted and treated piped water is regarded as the single most important determinant of public health, the litres per capita per day for each village was collected and analysed to the tune of the four classifications. The analysis of supply of drinking water in tandem with rural roads can be found in studies of Atagher and Atagher (2014), Eze (2012), and Olagunju et al. (2012).

Table 3.13 shows the litres per capita per day (LPCD) of the villages tabulated according to the four classifications of connectivity status, main transport route, distance from AWR and road network.

In Classification I, it can be seen that villages with AWR have higher LPCD than villages not connected with it. The average for the former is 33.79 litres while it is 31.27 litres for the latter. It can also be seen that villages lying along the main transport route have higher LPCD than those that are not – their respective averages being 39.58 litres and 30.51 litres. However, distance from AWR shows a contrasting feature as villages outside 15 km of AWR has the highest average of LPCD at 33.86 litres while those within 15 km have 29.02 litres. On the other hand, villages with higher network of road have higher LPCD at 34.77 litres while those with lower network have an average of 31.05 litres per capita per day.

From the above interpretation, it can be seen that the amount of piped water supplied to the study areas was found to be greater in almost all of the cases in favour of the villages with better road connectivity. This can be assumed to have positive impacts on the economy as the supply of clean drinking water contributes to sustainable improvements in peoples' lives regarding their health and education situation, which are the preconditions for productive employment (Hesselbarth, 2005).

c) Health Care Facilities

The next set of investigation is of health care institutions. It is often stated that economic development contributes to better health care and vice versa (Cypher and Dietz, 2004). More elaborately, health improvement contributes to economic development by improving productivity and learning, reducing family size and even increasing availability of land for productive use. At the same time, access to health care facilities may be severely limited by the road connectivity status and transport services. Extensive research work regarding road connectivity and its impact on health care has been done by various authors like Banerjee and Sachdeva (2015), Ibrahim (2013), Bhatt and Joshi (2013), Bhandari and Dutta (2014), to name a few. As such, the inclusion of analysis of health care facilities present in villages for the present study may be justified.

The following tables (Table 3.14, Table 3.15, Table 3.16, and Table 3.17) show the number of health care facilities available in the rural areas which are again tabulated according to the four classifications.

In Table 3.14, it can be seen that all of the Community Health Centres (CHCs) of the rural areas are in villages connected with AWR while in Table 3.15,

Table 3.14: Classification I: Health Care Facilities

Sl. No.	Health Facilities	Number of Villages			Percentage of Villages		
		Connected with AWR	Not Connected with AWR	Total	Connected with AWR	Not Connected with AWR	Total
1	Community Health Centre	6	0	6	100	0	100
2	Primary Health Centre	36	5	41	87.80	12.20	100
3	Sub-Centre	117	95	212	55.19	44.81	100
4	Sub-Centre Clinic	27	29	56	48.21	51.79	100
5	No Health Facilities	84	118	202	41.58	58.42	100
	Total	270	247	517	52.22	47.78	100

Source: Field Survey, 2015

Table 3.15: Classification II: Health Care Facilities

Sl. No.	Health Facilities	Number of Villages			Percentage of Villages		
		Along Main Route	Outside Main Route	Total	Along Main Route	Outside Main Route	Total
1	Community Health Centre	5	1	6	83.33	16.67	100
2	Primary Health Centre	18	23	41	43.90	56.10	100
3	Sub-Centre	58	154	212	27.36	72.64	100
4	Sub-Centre Clinic	9	47	56	16.07	83.93	100
5	No Health Facilities	22	180	202	10.89	89.11	100
	Total	112	405	517	21.66	78.34	100

Source: Field Survey, 2015

Table 3.16: Classification III: Health Care Facilities

Sl. No.	Health Facilities	Number of Villages				Percentage of Villages			
		AWR	Within 15 km	Outside 15 km	Total	AWR	Within 15 km	Outside 15 km	Total
1	Community Health Centre	6	0	0	6	100	0	0	100
2	Primary Health Centre	36	1	4	41	87.80	2.44	9.76	100
3	Sub-Centre	117	45	50	212	55.19	21.23	23.58	100
4	Sub-Centre Clinic	27	14	15	56	48.21	25	26.79	100
5	No Health Facilities	84	72	46	202	41.58	35.64	22.77	100
	Total	270	132	115	517	52.22	25.53	22.24	100

Source: Field Survey, 2015

83.33 per cent are in villages along the main transport route and 16.67 per cent are in villages outside the route. As is already stated, CHCs are concentrated in villages with AWR, so there are no such facilities in villages within and outside 15 km of AWR (Table 3.16). However, in Table 3.17 when classification is done accounting for road network, the CHCs of the state are evenly distributed in villages with road network below and above 7.5 km. Therefore, it may be concluded that Community Health Centres are typically located in villages with

Table 3.17: Classification IV: Health Care Facilities

Sl. No.	Health Facilities	Number of Villages			Percentage of Villages		
		Below 7.5 km	Above 7.5 km	Total	Below 7.5 km	Above 7.5 km	Total
1	Community Health Centre	3	3	6	50	50	100
2	Primary Health Centre	6	35	41	14.63	85.37	100
3	Sub-Centre	118	94	212	55.66	44.34	100
4	Sub-Centre Clinic	33	23	56	58.93	41.07	100
5	No Health Facilities	144	58	202	71.29	28.71	100
	Total	304	213	517	58.80	41.20	100

Source: Field Survey, 2015

better road connectivity showing a significant relation between the availability of Community Health Centres and road connectivity.

It can also be seen that 87.80 per cent of Primary Health Centres (PHCs) are in the connected villages while 12.20 per cent are in villages not connected with AWR. However, the number of PHCs is higher in villages lying outside of the main transport route as 56.10 per cent are in these villages while the remaining 43.90 per cent are in villages along main route. Again, as 87.80 per cent of PHCs are in villages with AWR, the remaining are distributed among the other villages of which 9.76 per cent are in villages outside 15 km of AWR which is higher than in villages within 15 km of AWR at 2.44 per cent. According to the road network measure, 85.37 per cent are in villages with network above 7.5 km while 14.63 per cent are in villages with road network below 7.5 km. The data for Primary Health Centres thus give us a mixed result where the number is higher in villages with AWR connection and those with higher road network, while at the same time it is lower in villages along main route and villages within 15 km of AWR than their respective counterparts.

The study also found that there are more Sub-Centres in villages connected with AWR than in villages that are not connected as their percentages are 55.19 and 44.81 respectively. On the other hand, in the second classification, 72.64 per cent of sub-centres are in villages outside the main transport route while the same is 27.36 per cent for villages along the transport route. For villages farther than 15 km from AWR, the percentage is 23.58 which is slightly higher than for villages within 15 km at 21.23 per cent. It can also be seen that 55.66 per cent of Sub-Centres are in villages below 7.5 km road network while the remaining 44.34 per cent are in villages with road network above 7.5 km. Thus, it may be stated that Sub-Centres are concentrated in villages with poor road connectivity as it is true for almost all of the classifications.

The tables also show that 51.79 per cent of Sub-Centre Clinics are in villages not connected with AWR and 83.93 per cent in villages outside main transport route, which means that these Clinics are usually established in far-flung villages. Table 3.16 also shows that 26.79 per cent of Sub-Centre Clinics are in villages lying farther than 15 km from the nearest AWR while 25 per cent are in villages within 15 km. Along the same line, 58.93 per cent are in villages with road network below 7.5 km while the remaining 41.07 per cent are in villages with road network above 7.5 km, which means that there are more Sub-Centre Clinics in villages of lower road network. In a nutshell, it can be concluded that the number Sub-Centre Clinics is higher in villages with inferior road connectivity than in villages with better road connectivity.

There are more villages with no health care facility in the 'not connected with AWR' category of Classification I. These villages compose 58.42 per cent of the total number of villages without any health care facility while the rest are AWR-connected villages. At the same time, of the total number of villages in which there are no health care facilities, 89.11 per cent are villages outside the main transport route while 10.89 per cent are villages along the main route. For villages that are not connected with AWR, Classification III shows that villages within 15 km compose 35.64 per cent of the same measure and villages outside 15 km compose 22.77 per cent. It can also be seen from the table that out of the total, absence of health care facilities is more acute in lower road network villages as they compose 71.29 per cent while the remaining 28.71 per cent are villages with road network above 7.5 km. Therefore, it can be seen that although the number of Sub-Centres and Sub-Centre Clinics is higher in villages with poor road connectivity, the total number of villages without any health care facility is still higher in this broad classification than the number of villages classified as villages with better road connectivity.

In line with the number of health facilities in villages, the number of trained personnel and health care providers available was determined and then fitted for each village. Table 3.18 shows the average number of medical officers, nurses, and health workers present in the study area according to the four classifications.

First, with an overall average of 0.06 per village, the average number of doctors (per 1000 population) available in the AWR-connected villages is 0.09 which is significantly higher than villages not connected with AWR whose average is 0.02. The same can be observed in villages along the main transport route as the average is 0.10 while it is only 0.04 for those lying outside the route. However, although significantly lower than those connected with AWR, villages within

Table 3.18: Number of Health Care Personnel Available

Figures in Average

Classification	Cases	Doctors per 1000	Nurses per 1000	Health Workers per 1000
I Connectivity Status	Connected with AWR	0.09	0.26	1.51
	Not Connected with AWR	0.02	0.06	1.55
II Main Transport Route	Along Main Route	0.1	0.3	2.03
	Outside Main Route	0.04	0.12	1.39
III Distance from AWR	AWR	0.09	0.26	1.51
	Within 15 km	0.01	0.02	1.2
	Outside 15 km	0.03	0.1	1.94
IV Road Network	Below 7.5 km	0.03	0.09	1.47
	Above 7.5 km	0.09	0.26	1.6
	Total	0.06	0.16	1.53

Source: Field Survey, 2015

15 km of nearest AWR have lesser number of doctors than villages outside 15 km. Their averages are 0.01 and 0.03, respectively. In the classification according to network of road, villages with network of road above 7.5 km have a higher average (0.09) than villages with network below 7.5 km (0.03). As such, it may be concluded that villages with better road connectivity houses a larger number of doctors as the average for it is higher in most of the cases than the average for villages with poor road connectivity.

Second, it can be seen that the average number of nurses is higher in almost all the cases for villages with better road connectivity. While the state average is 0.16, the number of nurses per 1000 population in connected villages is 0.26 which is significantly higher than the average for villages not connected with AWR at 0.06. Likewise, the average number of nurses in villages along the main route (0.30) is higher than villages outside the main route (0.12). For villages not connected and are farther than 15 km from the nearest AWR, the average number of nurses is 0.10 while the same is 0.02 for villages within 15 km. It can also be seen that villages that possess road network higher than or equal to 7.5 km have higher number of nurses (0.26) per village than those with a road network below 7.5 km (0.09).

Lastly, the average number of health workers available in the study area for 1000 persons is 1.53. It can be seen from the table that AWR-connected villages have a lower number of health workers than those not connected with it, their respective averages being 1.51 and 1.55. In contrast, for villages along the main route, the number is 2.03 which is higher than the average for villages outside the main route at 1.39. For the third classification, villages outside 15 km have the highest average at 1.94 followed by those that are connected whose average, as already mentioned, is 1.51, and is the lowest in villages within 15 km of the nearest AWR with 1.20 health workers per village. Like that of the former two averages, the number of health workers is higher in villages with road network above 7.5 km as the average of it is 1.60 while it is 1.47 for villages with 7.5 km network of road. This data for the number of health care workers shows varied results across the classifications. While the average is higher in villages along the main road and villages with road network above 7.5 km, it is lower in villages with AWR connection and in villages within 15 km of AWR than their respective counterparts.

Concluding Remarks

The chapter shows the analysis of the study area through the adoption of various measures of road connectivity, namely, all weather road connection, location along the main transport route, distance from the nearest all weather road and the length of road network. These classifications are applied to check if there are significant differences in selected development parameters. The parameters selected for the study are demography, depicted through basic population characteristics; employment, as indicated by workers' details; agricultural development, as represented by land use; and availability of basic social infrastructures. The main conclusions based on these observations may be summarised as follows:

In the study of the population characteristics, villages having better road connectivity have better achievement with respect to population development in most of the cases. This is indicated by higher sex ratio and literacy rates. At the same time, although the average of the total number of population is higher in these villages, the size of the family is larger in villages with poor road connectivity.

With respect to employment as indicated by workers' detail, villages with better road connectivity can be identified as more developed because the percentage of workers to population and the percentage of main workers in particular are higher in these villages when taken in aggregate. It may, however, be noted that the percentage of agricultural labourers is significantly higher which may be due to unavailability of land in the areas. Another important point that needs to be acknowledged is the greater contribution of industrial activities among both the main and marginal workers of villages with better road connectivity. Meanwhile, in villages with poor road connectivity, the percentage of females to total workers is high in most of the classifications. Also higher in these villages is the percentage of cultivators in both the cases of main and marginal workers. In addition, the percentage of marginal workers is also higher in villages with poor road connectivity. This denotes the undeveloped state of agriculture through the mirror of mass practice of unsustainable shifting cultivation which is seasonal in nature.

Examination of the existing state of land utilisation for determining the status of agriculture development shows, firstly, that the area of wet rice cultivation is higher in villages with better road connectivity. Secondly, the fact that agricultural plantation area is higher in these villages denotes a favourable state of agriculture because it is a viable option when the topography of the state is taken into consideration. Thirdly, the area under forest cover is higher in villages with poor road connectivity, which is not surprising. Fourthly, the jhum size per family is higher in villages with poor road connectivity. This points to the fact that jhumming is practised at a more extensive level in these villages which is again in line with the low intensity of agricultural plantation area.

Moreover, the villages with better and poorer road connectivity show distinct performances in the analysis of basic social infrastructure as well. First, in most of the cases, the connected villages show better educational development which is measured through the number of schools per village and teacher-pupil ratio. Secondly, in provision of health service, analysis of the average number of health care facilities like CHCs, PHCs, Sub-Centres, and Clinics and the average number of doctors, nurses, and health workers per 1000 population shows a higher performance in villages with better road connectivity. Thirdly, in the measure of the availability of drinking water supply, these villages also show better performance.

However, it may be included that the analysis of socio-economic development through the four classifications shows mixed results in some of the parameters used in the study. Mention may be made of the countering results in population density, male workers' ratio to total workers, and the number of primary health centres.

At the same time, it was found in most of the cases that villages with better road connectivity status outperform their adversaries in the different development parameters identified in the study. Thus, it may be concluded that rural road connectivity is directly associated with development.

4

Impact of Road Connectivity on Rural Development: An Empirical Analysis

Introduction

Provision of adequate and quality infrastructure in rural areas is considered a *sine qua non* because it is crucial for agricultural, industrial, and overall economic development and incidentally provides basic amenities, which improve the quality of life (NABARD, 2004). Moreover, an extensive, adequate, and efficient rural feeder road network serves as one of the channels for the collection and movement of goods and services, movement of people, and dissemination of information. It helps in the exchange of rural productivity as well as strengthening the socio-economic, cultural, and political fabrics and processes of the rural communities (Umoren et al., 2009).

The aim is to examine the effect that road connectivity has on rural development in the villages of Mizoram. The exercise in the previous chapter gave us basic information about the assertion that connectivity is a determinant of development. In addition to these findings, it was felt necessary to undertake further empirical investigation so that a firm conclusion could be drawn. This chapter therefore attempts to present the relationship between road connectivity and rural development using a regression model.

But first, to have a clearer view on the differential performance of villages that have different connectivity status, t-test was adopted to test for significance of difference in the identified development parameters. It is important to note that the terminologies used in this chapter for the connectivity classifications are AWR Connectivity, Main Route, Distance, and Road Network. Like that of the previous chapter, here, 'AWR Connectivity' is the classification of villages on whether or not they are connected with all-weather roads and the 'Main Route' classification is of the villages on whether they lie along the main transport route of the state or not. The 'Distance' classification covers the distance of unconnected villages from the nearest AWR and categorised the villages into those within 15 km and those outside 15 km of the nearest AWR. Lastly, the 'Road Network' classification groups the villages according to the length of roads in the villages – those with road network below and above 7.5 km.

Testing significance of differences can be found in the literature of various researchers in their study of rural road's impact on development. While Huang and Hsieh (2014) used correlation analysis to test the level of significance of their observations, t-test was applied by Umoren et al. (2009) and Mu and van de Walle (2007) for examining differences of means in their respective studies. At the same time, difference-in-difference method was adopted by Lokshin and Yemtsov (2005) and Kiprono and Matsumoto (2014), while Dorosh et al. (2012), Olagunju et al. (2012), and Freitas et al. (2009) tested the relationships of variables using regression analysis.

The rest of the chapter is divided into three parts. The first one shows the t-test of difference in performance, the second presents the estimation of the regression model and the third gives the concluding observations.

Testing the Difference in Performances

The main thrust of the analysis is to examine whether there are significant differences in the development parameters between the villages that have different connectivity status. This can primarily be taken as the impact of road connectivity on their economic condition. To come to this, t-test for difference of means has been appropriated to examine the average performance of villages across the different classifications presented in the last chapter.

The statistic adopted in the study may be defined as follows:

$$t = \frac{\bar{x}_1 - \bar{x}_2}{\sqrt{s^2\left(\frac{1}{n_1} + \frac{1}{n_2}\right)}}$$

where $\bar{x}_1$ and $\bar{x}_2$ are mean in area 1 and area 2 respectively, and

$$s^2 = \frac{1}{n_1 + n_{2-2}}\left[\sum (x_{1i} - \bar{x}_1)^2 + \sum (x_{2j} - \bar{x}_2)^2\right]$$

which follows students' t-distribution with $n_1 + n_2 - 2$ degrees of freedom.

The results and observations of the t-test for difference of performance are presented in the following sub-sections:

Population Development

The first set of parameters of economic development adopted in the study is the population structure of the rural areas as obtained from the Population Census 2011. This may be interpreted as the 'quality' of the population. Table 4.1 presents the structure of population of the study area.

The table shows that the t-statistic is significant for the classification of 'AWR Connectivity' in most of the cases except Population Density, Sex Ratio, and Child Sex Ratio. A similar trend can be seen in the 'Main Route' classification and 'Road Network' classification. This means that there are significantly different population structures between the respective categories of these classifications i.e., between the villages connected and not connected with AWR (AWR Connectivity classification), between villages along main transport route and outside main route (Main Route classification) and between villages with higher and lower road network (Road Network classification). In other words, villages having different connectivity statuses have shown significantly different structures of population. This can be construed as an impact of road connectivity.

It was observed in the previous chapter that villages connected with AWR, villages along the main road, and villages with higher road network (villages with

Table 4.1: Testing of Difference in Population Quality

Sl. No.	Variable	t-Value for Difference of Means			
		AWR Connectivity	Main Route	Distance	Road Network
1	Total Population	6.20***	6.48***	0.82	7.99***
2	Population Density	1.44	-0.25	2.44*	-1.22
3	Sex Ratio	1.20	0.61	-1.16	1.90
4	Child - Population Ratio	-7.26***	-6.46***	-0.36	-6.85***
5	Child Sex Ratio	-0.06	0.65	-0.47	1.04
6	Number of households	6.62***	7.24***	0.86	8.41***
7	Family Size	-3.56***	-5.14***	-0.33	-3.77***
8	Literacy Rate	5.23***	5.47***	-0.95	7.24***
9	Female Literacy Rate	5.10***	5.43***	-1.12	7.20***

*** - significant at all levels, ** - significant at 1%, * - significant at 5%

better road connectivity, for short) showed favourable situations. Therefore, we may conclude that road connectivity leads to significant differences between villages with better road connectivity and those with poor connectivity status, favouring the former. However, it can be observed that the 'Distance' classification (i.e. distance of village from the nearest AWR) does not show significant differences on the population development between the two categories of villages under it.

Employment Distribution

The second set of development parameter tested for the study is how employment is distributed in the villages. In other words, it accounted for the economic activities of the population, which is represented by the composition of workers. The calculated t-statistic for mean differences of these indicators across the four classifications is shown in Table 4.2.

In the classification of villages on whether they are connected with AWR, the t-statistic is significant at all levels for agricultural labourers (marginal)

Table 4.2: Testing of Difference in Workers' Composition

Sl. No.	Variable	t-Value for Difference of Means			
		AWR Connectivity	Main Route	Distance	Road Network
1	Percentage of Workers to Total Population	1.15	2.20*	0.52	3.10**
2	Workers' Sex Ratio	-0.98	-0.39	-1.66	0.71
3	Main Workers (% to Total Workers)	2.41*	0.67	2.05*	1.68
	Cultivators	*-2.11**	*-3.99****	*1.72*	*-0.31*
	Agricultural Labourers	*3.06***	*4.33****	*0.20*	*0.68*
	Household Industry Workers	*0.59*	*1.03*	*-1.15*	*2.43**
4	Marginal Workers (% to Total Workers)	-1.68	-0.36	-1.58	-0.82
	Cultivators	*-1.26*	*-1.24*	*-1.13*	*-0.53*
	Agricultural Labourers	*4.70****	*5.12****	*0.02*	*2.18**
	Household Industry Workers	*0.39*	*0.99*	*-0.82*	*1.59*

*** - significant at all levels, ** - significant at 1%, * - significant at 5%

while that of the main workers is significant at one per cent. At the same time, the table suggests that a mere connection with AWR does not translate into the improvement in the percentage of workers in the total population, workers' sex ratio, and percentage of marginal workers. It is interesting to note that AWR connectivity has affected the prevalence of agricultural labourers, for main workers as well as marginal workers, acknowledging the significant t-statistic and the higher percentage averaged in this category as shown in the previous chapter.

The locational status of the villages i.e. along the main transport route or outside, have shown little impact on the composition of workers excepting cultivators, agricultural labourers, and total workers. Meanwhile, the other two measures adopted as connectivity parameters in the study, namely Distance from AWR and Road Network, were found to have hardly impacted the quality of workers' composition as the t-statistic are insignificant in majority of the cases.

Agricultural Land Use

The third parameter of rural development identified for the study is agricultural development, which is derived from the land use patterns of villages. Table 4.3 shows land use data tested against t-statistic.

The t-test shows that the statistic is significant at all levels for agricultural plantation area, average jhum area per household, and area within 1 km of

Table 4.3: Difference in the Indicators of Rural Land Use

Sl. No.	Variable	t-Value for Difference of Means			
		AWR Connectivity	Main Route	Distance	Road Network
1	Percentage of WRC Area	0.09	-0.70	1.45	-1.71
2	Percentage of Agriculture Plantation Area	4.79***	5.56***	-0.48	4.86***
3	Percentage of Forest Area	-2.36*	0.57	-1.61	0.65
4	Average Jhum Area per Household (ha)	-4.81***	-5.97***	-0.62	0.299
5	Geographical Area of the Village	0.61	1.43	-2.10*	6.98***
6	Area within 1 km from motorable road	11.44***	8.71***	2.70**	27.23***

*** - significant at all levels, ** - significant at 1%, * - significant at 5%

motorable road for the 'AWR Connectivity' and 'Main Route' classifications, while for the 'Road Network' classification, it is significant at the same level for agriculture plantation area and total area of the village. This denotes that classifications according to whether or not they are connected with AWR and whether they lie along the main route show results of significant differences across their respective categories for plantation area, jhum area, and area of village within 1 km of motorable road. Thus, the condition that it is being connected with AWR and / or that it lies along the main transport route results in a favourable state for the village which can be interpreted as agricultural development because a larger area of agricultural plantation and a smaller area of jhum cover was observed in the analysis undertaken in the previous chapter. These villages also have a larger area within motorable road which can translate into higher opportunities for agricultural marketing.

It may also be noted that a higher agricultural plantation area was observed in villages with higher road network. The highly significant difference in average jhum size per household shows a more extensive practice of traditional jhum system in the villages with poor connectivity. We can, therefore, conclude that the average performance of the villages having better connectivity conditions is significantly higher with respect to agricultural development. However, the classification of villages according to their distance from the nearest AWR does not show any significant difference between its categories. Thus, we can say that the distance of the village from AWR does not have a noteworthy impact on agricultural development, so also for land use.

Availability of Social Amenities

The availability of basic social infrastructures was adopted as a parameter of development as well. The social infrastructures under study are educational facilities and its personnel, the supply of piped drinking water and availability of health care institutions and qualified medical personnel. First, the test of difference for educational institutions is presented in Table 4.4.

The table (Table 4.4) shows that t-statistic is significant at all levels in all the variables for AWR Connectivity, Main Route, and Road Network classifications. This implies that within the categories of these classifications, there are significant differences in the availability of educational institutions – from Primary to Higher Secondary levels. We can, therefore, conclude that villages having better connectivity conditions outperform villages with poor road connectivity in the contest of availability of educational institutions as it is higher for these villages (also presented in Chapter 3). On the other hand, it can be seen that the classification of

Table 4.4: Test of Difference for Availability of Educational Institutions

Sl. No.	Variables	t-Value for Difference of Means			
		AWR Connectivity	Main Route	Distance	Road Network
1	No. of Primary Schools	5.85***	6.04***	-0.62	7.68***
2	No. of Middle Schools	5.80***	6.77***	1.07	7.76***
3	No. of High Schools	6.85***	6.32***	0.44	6.81***
4	No. of Higher Secondary Schools	4.07***	3.96***	0.36	5.00***
5	Total No. of Schools	6.80***	7.14***	0.16	8.56***

*** - significant at all levels

Table 4.5: Test on the Availability of Educators

Sl. No.	Variable	t-Value for Difference of Means			
		AWR Connectivity	Main Route	Distance	Road Network
1	Primary School Teacher-Student Ratio	1.77	1.19	-0.82	1.06
2	Middle School Teacher-Student Ratio	-0.07	-0.15	-0.13	1.05
3	High School Teacher-Student Ratio	4.57***	3.36**	0.16	4.39***
4	Higher Secondary Teacher-Student Ratio	4.08***	3.90***	-0.55	5.01***
5	Total Teacher-Student Ratio	1.23	1.01	-0.86	1.57

*** - significant at all levels, ** - significant at 1%

villages according to their distance from the nearest AWR does not seem to result in significant differences among its categories (within 15 km and outside 15 km).

In line with the above, Table 4.5 shows the availability of educators. Here, the denotation for the teacher-student ratio is the number of teachers present for 100 students.

It can be derived from the table that, on an average, villages with better road connectivity have a significantly higher performance in the development of secondary education. It is shown that the test is significant at all levels for the average number of teachers per 100 students in high schools and higher secondary schools for the classification of 'AWR Connectivity.' A more or less similar trend can be seen in 'Main Route' and 'Road Network' classifications. Therefore, the status of a village that it is connected with AWR, that it lies along the main transport route and that it has a greater road network has higher teacher-student ratio than its respective counterparts, which would result in a higher quality of secondary education, the reasoning of which was explained in the previous chapter. In contrast, the availability of teachers in favourable numbers is not affected by distance of the village from nearest AWR as the t-statistic is insignificant for all the levels of schooling.

Another infrastructure tested is the amount of piped drinking water supplied in the village. The t-test for amount of water supply is shown in Table 4.6.

The t-statistic for amount of supply of piped drinking water is not significant for the various classifications of road connectivity except on 'Main Route' classification i.e., whether the village lies along the main transport route of the state, where it is significant at one per cent level.

In addition to water supply and educational institutions and personnel, the availability of health personnel in the villages was also tested. The t-statistic for it is presented in Table 4.7.

Table 4.6: Test on Amount of Water Supply

Sl. No.	Classification	t-Value for Difference of Means
1	AWR Connectivity	1.[illegible]5
2	Main Route	3.43**
3	Distance	-1.92
4	Road Network	1.77

** - significant at 1%

Table 4.7: Test on the Availability of Qualified Medical Personnel

Sl. No.	Variables	t-Value for Difference of Means			
		AWR Connectivity	Main Route	Distance	Road Network
1	No. of Doctors	3.83***	2.79**	-1.45	3.15**
2	No. of Nurses	3.85***	2.79**	-1.45	3.36**
3	No. of Health Workers	-0.11	1.48	-2.32*	0.36

*** - significant at all levels, ** - significant at 1%, * - significant at 5%

The table shows that the average performance of the villages having better connectivity conditions is significantly higher with respect to availability of health care personnel, particularly doctors and nurses. Here, the t-statistic for the two types of personnel is significant at all levels for the classification of 'AWR Connectivity' while for the 'Main Route' and 'Road Network' classifications, it is significant at one per cent. However, none is significant for the 'Distance' classification except for the number of health workers which is significant negatively at five per cent level. Nevertheless, it can be inferred from the findings of the test that villages with better road connectivity conditions have a significantly higher number of qualified medical personnel in their villages.

Lastly, with respect to health care facilities, the institutions being considered in the study are Primary Health Centres, Community Health Centres, Sub-Centres, and Sub-Centre Clinics. It is important to note that normally, these institutions are not available in all the villages and even in those villages that they are, only one is generally established. So, the only option for testing the difference is to test the frequency difference. Consequently, the chi-square test of independence of attributes was found suitable for this test. This is defined as –

$$\chi^2 = \sum \left[\frac{(O_i - E_i)^2}{E_i} \right]$$

where Oi = Number of villages observed to have such health care institution, and
Ei = Expected number of villages to have such institution,

which follows chi-square distribution with (r – 1) (c – 1) degrees of freedom. (r = no. of rows, c = no. of columns)

The result is presented in Table 4.8 in which the chi-square value is significant for 'AWR connectivity' classification, 'Main Route' classification, and 'Road Network' classification. This means that the classification of a village on whether it is connected with AWR or not, whether it lies along the main transport route

Table 4.8: Test on Availability of Health Care Institutions

Sl. No.	Classification	Chi-Square Value	Significance
1	AWR Connectivity	36.56	0.000
2	Main Route	44.29	0.000
3	Distance	6.68	0.083
4	Road Network	47.07	0.000

or not and its network of road network results in significant differences between their categories on the availability of health care institutions.

It can, therefore, be concluded that the performance of the villages having better connectivity conditions is significantly higher with respect to these facilities. On the other hand, it has been observed that the 'Distance' classification (i.e. distance of village from AWR) does not result in significant differences for the availability of health care institutions.

Relationship Between Road Connectivity and Rural Development – A Regression Model

To examine the relationship between road connectivity and development, it is attempted to fit a regression equation where the developmental parameters are taken as dependent variables and the connectivity measures as independent variables or regressor. As the AWR connectivity variable is qualitative or categorical in nature, the normal classical regression model could not be applied. Consequently, the study decided to adopt Dummy Variable Regression Model which comprises development variables as dependent variables, and the qualitative (which takes the value 1 and 0) and quantitative connectivity variables as the explanatory variables.

To explain this further, the two connectivity variables, namely road network and distance from the nearest AWR can be quantified in kilometres. The variable of AWR connectivity is categorical in nature and thus, the values 1 and 0 were assigned for connected and unconnected villages respectively; while the same is the case for the location of the village on whether it lies along the main road or not. However, the status of the village whether it is located along the main road was found to be overlapping with its status on AWR connectivity because those located along the main route are connected by AWR. There will, therefore, be a problem called *dummy variable trap* if both are simultaneously introduced in the same model. It was thus decided to exclude the dummy variable of main route, while adopting the AWR connectivity dummy as it has better significance of difference in most of the cases. In addition, AWR connectivity is the most commonly accepted indicator of rural road connectivity in economic literature (Parida, 2014; Ibok and Daniel, 2013; Ulimwengu et al., 2009; Mu and van de Walle, 2007; Khandker et al., 2006).

As two of the independent variables are quantitative while one is qualitative in nature having values of 1 and 0 only, it is appropriate to use Analysis of Covariance (ANOCOVA) dummy regression model. In most economic research, a regression model contains some explanatory variables that are quantitative and some that are qualitative (Gujarati et al., 2012). Thus, the following regression model was estimated:

$$Y_i = \beta_0 + \beta_1 D_{1i} + \beta_2 X_{1i} + \beta_3 X_{2i} + U_i$$

where Y_i = Development variable of interest obtained from the villages.

β_0 = Intercept term

D_{1i} = 1, if the village is connected with AWR
= 0, otherwise

X_{1i} = Road Network (km)

X_{2i} = Distance of Village from nearest AWR (km).

U_i = Error term

Since three explanatory variables are being used in the model, the problem of multicollinearity should be a matter of concern. To measure the presence or degree of multicollinearity, the Condition Index (CI) given by –

$$CI = \sqrt{\frac{Maximum\ Eigenvalue}{Minimum\ Eigenvalue}}$$

was adopted with the following rule of thumb: (i) if $10 \le CI \le 30$, there is moderate to strong multicollinearity, (ii) if $CI > 30$, there is strong multicollinearity, and (iii) if $CI < 10$, there is weak or low multicollinearity.

In the process of estimating the regression model, it was observed that the R-Square as a ratio of explained variation to the total variation were found to be very low in many of the cases even though the estimated coefficients are highly significant with a highly significant F-statistic. It should be remembered that connectivity is in fact only one of the determinants of economic development of a village. For example, it is the size of the population, rather than the status of road connectivity, that normally determines the demand for provision of basic social amenities like schools, medical institutions, etc. in countries like India. Since this is the case, the main concern is to test if the connectivity variable is a significant estimator of development and the overall significance of the model measured through F-statistic.

The estimated regression models to each major development variable are presented in the following sub-sections.

Relationship Between Road Connectivity and Population Quality

Table 4.9 shows the result of estimated regression of population quality on road connectivity.

The calculated condition index (CI) is 4.83 and is in the acceptable range. Table 4.9 shows that the calculated F-statistics are significant in all cases except for

Table 4.9: Estimated Regression of the Population Development on Road Connectivity

Sl. No.	Dependent Variable	Constant	Coefficient of Independent Variables			R-square	F- Statistic
			AWR Connectivity	Road Network	Distance		
1	Total Population	593.50	250.92	34.53	3.35	0.174	35.92
		(0.000)	(0.015)	(0.000)	(0.313)		(0.000)
2	Population Density	61.30	88.30	-4.78	-0.70	0.012	2.02
		(0.200)	(0.126)	(0.048)	(0.706)		(0.110)
3	Sex Ratio	923.09	20.00	0.79	0.94	0.024	4.16
		(0.000)	(0.048)	(0.061)	(0.004)		(0.006)
4	Child-Population Ratio	194.07	-14.97	-0.66	0.10	0.118	22.96
		(0.000)	(0.001)	(0.000)	(0.462)		(0.000)
5	Child Sex Ratio	974.38	-41.51	5.27	0.30	0.037	6.64
		(0.000)	(0.143)	(0.000)	(0.741)		(0.000)
6	No. of Households	114.77	55.17	7.23	0.70	0.190	40.16
		(0.000)	(0.008)	(0.000)	(0.288)		(0.000)
7	Family Size	5.09	-0.09	-0.01	0.00	0.046	8.16
		(0.000)	(0.162)	(0.001)	(0.938)		(0.000)
8	Literacy Rate	62.52	5.74	0.40	0.06	0.088	16.44
		(0.000)	(0.007)	(0.000)	(0.391)		(0.000)
9	Female Literacy Rate	57.47	6.84	0.49	0.07	0.085	15.84
		(0.000)	(0.009)	(0.000)	(0.399)		(0.000)

1) Figure in bracket indicates significance level

2) Condition Index (CI) as indicator on the presence of multicollinearity equals 4.83

Population Density, though R-square is comparatively low in all cases. This suggests the significance of the estimated regression equation of population development on road connectivity. Meanwhile, as the overall regression is not significant, population density is not significantly related to road connectivity. This is in line with the observation given in the t-test of the preceding section. It can be observed that the coefficients of AWR connectivity are significant in most of the cases apart from Population Density, Child Sex Ratio, and Family Size. The positively significant coefficient implicates increasing population size, sex ratio, number of households, literacy rate, and female literacy rate with AWR connection while the negatively significant coefficient suggest the decline in child-population ratio with AWR connectivity of the village. Thus, it is safe to conclude that population development is directly associated with AWR connectivity by taking low dependency ratio (child-population ratio) as one of the development parameters.

The estimated coefficient on Road Network was found to be significant at five per cent level in most of the cases except for Sex Ratio, which is also significant at 10 per cent level. It is interesting to note that the coefficients are positive for Total Population, Sex Ratio, Child Sex Ratio, Number of Households, Literacy Rate, and Female Literacy Rate while it is negative for Population Density, Child-Population Ratio, and Family Size. It is thus clear that the increase in road network is strongly related to population development. However, the estimated coefficient of distance of the village from the nearest AWR, which otherwise may be taken as access to road communication throughout the year, was found to be significant only for Sex Ratio.

Relationship Between Road Connectivity and Composition of Workforce

Table 4.10 presents the estimated regression coefficient for various indicators of the structures of employment in the village on the three connectivity variables.

First, the calculated F-statistic as an indicator on the significance of the estimated regression is not significant for Workers' Sex Ratio, Household Industry Workers (Main), and Marginal Workers (Cultivators and Household Industry Workers). Moreover, the estimated R-square is very low in most of the cases, which suggests a weak impact of rural road connectivity in shaping the situation of employment and its composition in rural areas. This may otherwise be taken as low industrial development in rural areas of Mizoram which normally comes with the improvement of road infrastructure.

Second, it can be observed that the estimated coefficient of AWR Connectivity is insignificant for all major classification of workers, while it is

Table 4.10: Estimated Regression of the Composition of Workers on Road Connectivity

Sl. No.	Dependent Variable	Constant	Coefficient of Independent Variables			R-square	F- Statistic
			AWR Connectivity	Road Network	Distance		
1	Percentage of Workers to Total Population	49.41	-2.09	0.20	-0.08	0.033	5.80
		(0.000)	(0.132)	(0.001)	(0.076)		(0.001)
2	Workers' Sex Ratio	722.53	-16.93	1.67	0.99	0.007	1.82
		(0.000)	(0.575)	(0.184)	(0.310)		(0.316)
3	Percentage of Main Workers to Total Workers	89.96	-0.55	-0.02	-0.22	0.034	5.94
		(0.000)	(0.782)	(0.783)	(0.001)		(0.001)
	Cultivators	77.00	-6.62	-0.16	-0.19	0.020	3.45
		(0.000)	(0.020)	(0.169)	(0.035)		(0.016)
	Agriculture Labourers	3.04	1.84	0.12	-0.03	0.025	4.42
		(0.022)	(0.251)	(0.076)	(0.504)		(0.004)
	Household Industry Workers	0.36	0.05	0.01	0.00	0.007	1.21
		(0.012)	(0.789)	(0.088)	(0.453)		(0.304)
4	Percentage of Marginal Workers to Total Workers	5.58	-0.10	0.03	0.08	0.015	2.61
		(0.000)	(0.928)	(0.532)	(0.029)		(0.051)
	Cultivators	43.02	1.87	-0.03	0.31	0.011	1.93
		(0.000)	(0.697)	(0.891)	(0.044)		(0.123)
	Agricultural Labourers	8.81	8.48	0.09	-0.04	0.043	7.60
		(0.000)	(0.005)	(0.472)	(0.654)		(0.000)
	Household Industry Workers	2.53	-0.36	0.08	0.00	0.005	0.88
		(0.010)	(0.757)	(0.117)	(0.972)		(0.450)

Figure in bracket indicates significance level

significant for Cultivators (Main) and Agricultural Labourers (Marginal). The negatively significant Cultivators (Main) may implicate the situation that shifting cultivation remains the main provider of employment in the unconnected villages. At the same time, the significant estimate for Agricultural Labourers (Marginal) may imply scarcity of land for jhumming which compels many workers to work in other landowners' farms and also the practice of shifting cultivation as a mere subsidiary livelihood in the villages connected with AWR. This is in light of the observation that there are more areas of agriculture plantation in these villages.

Third, the estimated coefficients of Road Network are significant and positive for the percentage of Workers to Total Population and Agricultural Labourers showing their increase with the increasing road network. Lastly, the coefficient for Distance from AWR are significant for Main Workers, Cultivators (Main), Marginal Workers and Cultivators (Marginal). The negative coefficient for the percentage of Main Workers shows its decrease with the increase in the distance from AWR while the positive value for Marginal Workers suggests the increasing percentage of marginal workers with the declining distance from AWR.

Relationship between Road Connectivity and Agricultural Development

Table 4.11 shows the relationship between road connectivity and agricultural development as indicated by the dynamics of agricultural land use. This is measured by the estimated regression of agricultural land use on the three connectivity measures. It can be observed that the estimated regression is significant for all cases except the percentage of WRC area. Thus, one may state that road connectivity has significant contribution in the change in agricultural land use.

The coefficient of AWR connectivity for agriculture plantation is 0.16 which is significant at one per cent level. The coefficients for average jhum size per household and village area are -1.34 and -6.81, which are also significant at one per cent level. This result shows the practice of agriculture plantation at a more intense level in the villages connected by AWR and the increase in jhum size per household for villages not connected with AWR, which have a relatively lower geographical area. Thus, there is more practice of settled cultivation in AWR-connected villages while the shifting cultivation is more extensive in the unconnected villages.

The table also shows the significant impact of road network on agriculture as its estimated coefficients are significant for plantation, jhum size, and total geographical area of the village. The results indicate the coming up of agricultural

Table 4.11: Estimated Regression of the Agricultural Land Use on Road Connectivity

Sl. No.	Dependent Variable	Constant	Coefficient of Independent Variables			R-square	F- Statistic
			AWR Connectivity	Road Network	Distance		
1	Percentage of WRC Area	1.14	-0.05	-0.02	-0.01	0.007	1.12
		(0.000)	(0.882)	(0.142)	(0.226)		(0.339)
2	Percentage of Agriculture Plantation Area	0.07	0.16	0.01	0.00	0.056	10.06
		(0.173)	(0.018)	(0.010)	(0.805)		(0.000)
3	Percentage of Forest Area	73.27	-0.04	0.06	0.15	0.032	5.66
		(0.000)	(0.977)	(0.340)	(0.001)		(0.001)
4	Average Jhum Area per Household (ha)	4.42	-1.34	0.03	0.00	0.071	13.04
		(0.000)	(0.000)	(0.002)	(0.948)		(0.000)
5	Geographical Area of the Village	24.01	-6.81	1.76	0.37	0.340	88.18
		(0.000)	(0.010)	(0.000)	(0.000)		(0.000)

Figure in bracket indicates significance level

plantation with the increase in road network and also for jhum size, surprisingly. At the same time, the coefficient with respect to distance is significant for total geographical area of village only.

Relationship between Road Connectivity and the Availability of Basic Social Amenities

As noted earlier, the basic social amenities under study are availability of educational facilities and personnel, the amount of piped drinking water supplied, and the availability of health care institutions and trained medical personnel in the village.

First, Table 4.12 shows the result of estimated regression of educational facilities on road connectivity.

The significance of the estimated regression equation of educational facilities on road connectivity can be inferred as the calculated F-statistics are significant in all the dependent variables. It can be observed that the coefficients on AWR connectivity are significant in most of the cases except for number of Higher Secondary Schools. More specifically, the coefficient is positively significant at one per cent level for Primary Schools, High Schools, and the Total Number of Schools while it is significant at five per cent for the average number of Middle Schools. This implies that availability of educational institutions is positively associated with AWR connectivity. At the same time, the estimated coefficient on Road Network was found to be significant at all levels for all the cases thus showing the greatest difference-inducing capacity among the classifications under study. This gives an impression that increase in road network is strongly related to this factor of educational development. However, the estimated coefficient of the village's distance from the nearest AWR is not significant for any of the levels of educational institutions.

Second is the estimated regression of educational personnel / teachers on road connectivity. As is shown in Table 4.13, the estimated regression is significant for cases of Middle School, High Schools and Higher Secondary School. This may indicate that road connectivity does have a significant effect on the availability of a higher number of educational personnel.

It can be observed that the estimated coefficient of AWR Connectivity is significant at five per cent for high school level of education while the coefficient for Distance from AWR is insignificant for all levels. On the other hand, the estimated coefficient of Road Network was found to be significant at all levels for higher secondary while it is significant at one per cent level for middle school and 10 per cent for high school. Therefore, among the three, what can be stated as one of the factors influencing the availability of educational personnel and that

Table 4.12: Estimated Regression of Educational Institutions on Road Connectivity

Sl. No.	Dependent Variable	Constant	Coefficient of Independent Variables			R-square	F- Statistic
			AWR Connectivity	Road Network	Distance		
1	No. of Primary Schools	1.34	0.56	0.07	0.01	0.161	32.86
		(0.000)	(0.009)	(0.000)	(0.105)		(0.000)
2	No. of Middle Schools	1.11	0.29	0.04	0.00	0.144	28.73
		(0.000)	(0.037)	(0.000)	(0.647)		(0.000)
3	No. of High Schools	0.31	0.27	0.02	0.00	0.129	25.34
		(0.000)	(0.001)	(0.000)	(0.828)		(0.000)
4	No. of Higher Secondary Schools	0.00	0.04	0.01	0.00	0.069	12.65
		(0.934)	(0.206)	(0.000)	(0.917)		(0.000)
5	Total Number of Schools	2.76	1.16	0.13	0.01	0.185	38.86
		(0.000)	(0.004)	(0.000)	(0.284)		(0.000)

Figure in bracket indicates significance level

Table 4.13: Estimated Regression of Educational Personnel on Road Connectivity

Sl. No.	Dependent Variable	Constant	Coefficient of Independent Variables			R-square	F- Statistic
			AWR Connectivity	Road Network	Distance		
1	Primary School Teacher-Student Ratio	5.91	0.53	0.00	-0.01	0.006	1.10
		(0.000)	(0.304)	(0.930)	(0.656)		(0.347)
2	Middle School Teacher-Student Ratio	14.65	-2.57	0.18	-0.05	0.018	3.11
		(0.000)	(0.101)	(0.005)	(0.363)		(0.026)
3	High School Teacher-Student Ratio	6.79	3.92	0.12	-0.01	0.045	8.14
		(0.000)	(0.011)	(0.065)	(0.898)		(0.000)
4	Higher Secondary Teacher-Student Ratio	-0.34	0.47	0.10	0.01	0.092	17.42
		(0.310)	(0.252)	(0.000)	(0.682)		(0.000)
5	Total Teacher-Student Ratio	9.75	0.04	0.03	-0.02	0.006	1.05
		(0.000)	(0.959)	(0.345)	(0.432)		(0.368)

Figure in bracket indicates significance level

of the institutions is the increase in road network in which the size of population is incidentally higher (as shown in the previous chapter).

Third, the calculated F-Statistic as an indicator on the significance of the estimated regression of amount of piped water supply on road connectivity was found to be insignificant (0.272) and so, is not shown.

The fourth social amenity tested is the availability of qualified medical personnel in the village. The relationship of this with that of road connectivity is shown in Table 4.14 where the estimated regression is significant for all cases. It may, therefore, be stated that a significant relationship exists between road connectivity and availability of doctors, nurses, and health workers in the village.

The coefficients of AWR connectivity for Doctors and Nurses are 0.06 and 0.18 which are both significant at five per cent level. Also significant at five per cent is 'Health Workers,' which has a negative coefficient. This means that while there are more doctors and nurses in villages connected with AWR, health workers tend to be more concentrated in villages not connected with AWR. This is in line with the observation of the previous chapter.

It is also shown that there is an impact of road network on this development variable as its estimated coefficients are significant at all levels for Health Workers, at one per cent for Nurses and at five per cent level for Doctors. The positively significant coefficients of Road Network imply that the availability of medical personnel is strongly related to the concentration of road network of the village. However, no significant differences can be seen in the coefficients of Distance from AWR.

Concluding Remarks

It can be observed from the t-test for the significance of difference between the villages with better road connectivity and poor road connectivity that there is a significant difference between the two areas in most of the key development parameters, where the former is endowed with favourable conditions. Similarly, the estimated regressions are also significant in most of the cases as indicated by the significant F-Statistic, though R-Square is relatively low. A clear conclusion that could be drawn from this is that road connectivity is indeed a significant factor for economic development. This is in line with the findings of several researchers (Parida, 2014; Ibok and Daniel, 2013; Ulimwengu et al., 2009; Umoren et al., 2009; Oraboune, 2008; Mu and van de Walle, 2007; Khandker et al., 2006). The following summarises some of the notable points of the analyses:

First, the well-connected villages are richer with several attributes of population development than their counterpart i.e., unconnected villages. This is

Table 4.14: Estimated Regression of Availability of Qualified Medical Personnel on Road Connectivity

Sl. No.	Dependent Variable	Constant	Coefficient of Independent Variables			R-square	F- Statistic
			AWR Connectivity	Road Network	Distance		
1	No. of Doctors	-0.01 (0.778)	0.06 (0.011)	0.003 (0.013)	0.00 (0.266)	0.041	7.26 (0.000)
2	No. of Nurses	-0.02 (0.761)	0.18 (0.011)	0.01 (0.008)	0.00 (0.239)	0.043	7.65 (0.000)
3	No. of Health Workers	0.90 (0.023)	-1.11 (0.020)	0.15 (0.000)	0.01 (0.475)	0.096	18.09 (0.000)

Figure in bracket indicates significance level

evident from the higher literacy rate and female literacy rate, while observing lower family size with less child dependency as indicated by low child-population ratio, which is a basic characteristic of more advanced societies across the world. The significance and the sign of estimated regression coefficient suggest the tendency of this measure to move in this direction with the improvement in road connectivity.

Second, the study observed the situation where the composition of employment (workers' composition) is hardly impacted by road connectivity in most of the cases. However, an interesting observation is the increase of agricultural labourers with better connectivity situation, which suggests the existence of land scarcity where the poor landless suffer.

Third, with respect to the status of agricultural development, the study observed a higher prevalence of settled cultivation in the form of agricultural plantation in the well-connected villages whereas jhumming is practised more extensively in unconnected villages because the average jhum size per household is significantly higher in the latter cases. The sign of regression coefficients implicate the increasing trends of plantation areas with connectivity improvement and at the same time, the increasing jhum size with poor connectivity. It may be noted that it is an all-time objective of the state government to replace the unsustainable practice of traditional jhumming by settled cultivation, which is considered more sustainable and profitable, for development of the agriculture sector of the state. Thus, we may conclude that agriculture development is directly associated with connectivity.

Fourth, in spite of the fact that villages having better connectivity are having a larger population size vis-à-vis the notion that demand for availability of basic social infrastructure is determined by population, the study did observe a situation where well-connected villages are better endowed with such infrastructures. In fact, the availability of educational facilities in terms of infrastructure and manpower is more or less the same in the two areas for primary education. However, the availability of educational infrastructure for middle school and above is significantly higher in the connected villages than in the unconnected ones. It may be noted that the scarcity of teachers in the villages may result in school dropouts in the poorly connected villages. Therefore, the significant estimated regression coefficient of AWR connectivity and teacher-student ratio for middle school and high school should be a matter of concern keeping in view the objective of National Policy on Education, 1992, which aims at universal access to elementary education.

Fifth, a notable feature on the availability of social infrastructure is the significantly different number of qualified medical staff between the well-connected and poorly connected villages. In fact, the number of health workers (who run health sub-centres) is not significantly different between the two areas. However, the existence of health sub-centres under the supervision of health workers in the village does not necessarily translate into access to institutional health care because they are entrusted only for vaccination of children and pregnant women, while institutional child delivery can be done only in institutions where doctors and nurses are present. At the same time, the availability of doctors and nurses in the well-connected villages are significantly higher. Thus, it is safe to conclude that well-connected villages have better performance in terms of medical facilities.

Lastly, it would be an academic interest to address the comparatively low R-square of the estimated regression model, even for different types of regression models. At the same time, the significance of the calculated F-statistic with moderately low presence of multicollinearity should be interpreted as the model where the explanatory variables do have a significant impact on the dependent variables. The explanatory variable introduced in the model may be only one group of significant factors among other factors, while we cannot rule out the possibility of sequential process on the impact of road connectivity on development, e.g. connectivity improves the availability of educational infrastructure, which would further led to an improvement in population quality (literacy, etc.). Nevertheless, based on the significance of estimated regression, it is safe to conclude that road connectivity is undoubtedly a significant factor for development in rural areas.

5

Conclusion

Introduction

The primary objective is to examine the impact of road connectivity on rural development. While the development indicators are clubbed under four major heads, namely, population quality, composition of workers, agricultural land use, and availability of basic social infrastructures, the study adopted four connectivity variables comprising of AWR connectivity (whether the village is connected with AWR or not), main transport route (whether the village lies along the main transport route of the state), distance of the village from the nearest AWR and the network of road within the village. However, due to the apparent endogeneity of the key connectivity variables when taken as explanatory variables, it was found rather difficult to assess the direct impact of road connectivity on development. For example, the provision of basic social infrastructures in a democratic set-up is normally in places where the number of residents is high. These infrastructures usually enhance the quality of the population through increased literacy and the like. Therefore, the viable methodology to analyse the impact of road connectivity is to examine the differences in development levels between the well-connected and poorly connected villages in terms of these connectivity variables. This has been done using t-test for difference of means.

In addition to this, dummy variable regression model was adopted to enable us to analyse the changing pattern of development due to change in connectivity status. Of the four connectivity variables introduced, AWR connectivity was found to be having the most significant effect as it showed stark differences between its two categories – villages connected with AWR and those that are not. As such, the findings presented in the following gave emphasis on this connectivity variable.

This chapter presents the key findings and observations. The rest of the chapter is divided into three sections titled General Trend of Road Connectivity and Economic Development, Analytical Results of the Impact of Road Connectivity on Rural Development, and Conclusion and Recommendations.

General Trend of Road Connectivity and Economic Development

Accounting for the different levels of road connectivity infrastructure present across the states of India and that of their performances in different socio-economic indicators, those that have infrastructures better than the national average are also the states that have higher than average performances in various demographic and socio-economic development indicators like high literacy rates and child sex ratio, and low infant mortality rate. Moreover, households availing banking services and those with latrine facilities within the premises were also higher in the states with high density of road connectivity.

The total length of roads in Mizoram is 7548.029 km of which 4776.823 km (63.28 per cent) is surfaced. Here, the national and state highways (986.530 km and 310.450 km, respectively) are surfaced while for district roads and town roads, the percentage of surfaced roads are respectively 84.84 per cent and 85.13 per cent. Of all the types of roads in Mizoram, the worst are of village roads, where only 984.06 km (36.11 per cent) out of the total length of 2625.55 km are surfaced. Moreover, only 52.22 per cent of the villages are connected with all-weather roads (AWR).

The Total Plan Budget of Mizoram during the last ten years (2004-05 to 2013-14) grew at the rate of 14.45 per cent. However, the calculated compound annual growth rate (CAGR) for the transport sector as a whole is –3.53 per cent while for roads and road transport in particular, the CAGR is –3.73 per cent. At the same time, the CAGR of number of all types of vehicles for the period of 2010 to 2014 is 14.22 per cent.

A district-wise analysis of AWR connectivity status showed that while at least half of the villages in districts of Mamit, Kolasib, Aizawl, Champhai, and Lunglei are AWR-connected, Serchhip, Lawngtlai, and Saiha districts have less than 50 per cent of their villages connected with all-weather roads. It was also found that the district with the highest percentage of its villages connected with AWR is Kolasib at 75.86 per cent while it is the lowest in Saiha district as only 28.57 per cent of its villages are connected.

The percentage of villages along the main transport route, described here as the national highways, state highways, and roads connecting major transport destinations, is 21.66 per cent. Aizawl district ranks the highest with 44.30 per cent of its total villages along the main route while Lawngtlai district is at the bottom, as only 6.06 per cent of its total villages lie along the main transport route of the state.

The average road network of the villages of Mizoram was found to be 7.55 km. Adopting this as a demarcation, there are 304 villages with road network below this average and 213 above it. This means that 58.80 per cent of villages have road network lower than 7.5 km while 41.20 per cent have network of road that is higher than 7.5 km. Moreover, 132 of the villages not connected with AWR (i.e., 53.44 per cent) were found to be within 15 km of the nearest AWR while 115 villages (46.56 per cent) are farther than 15 km of the nearest AWR.

Analysis of the villages with the different connectivity variables introduced in the study and their status of demography showed that villages with better road connectivity have better achievement with respect to population development in most of the cases. An example may be cited of the literacy rate where AWR-connected villages have a per village average of 73.98 per cent while for those not connected, the average percentage is 64.85. Similar patterns were found in the other connectivity variables as well.

Mention may also be made of sex ratio whose average is higher in villages with better road connectivity. In AWR-connected villages, there are 952 females per 1000 males while in those not connected with AWR, the average is 944. On the other hand, the ratio of children to total population was found to be higher in villages with poor road connectivity. The percentage for unconnected villages is 19.40 per cent while it is 17.13 per cent for connected villages. This means that there are more children in villages with poor road connectivity that rely on others, which can be translated as higher dependency ratios in these villages.

In consonance with the total number of population which is higher in the villages with better road connectivity, the average number of households is also higher in these villages. The AWR connectivity classification showed that the average number of households for connected villages is 255 while it is only 150 for the unconnected ones. However, the size of the family is larger in villages with poor road connectivity. It was found that the average family size for villages not connected with AWR is 5.06 while connected villages have an average family size of 4.90.

With respect to employment as indicated by workers' composition, villages with better road connectivity can be identified as being more developed because the percentage of workers to population and the percentage of main workers in particular are higher in these villages when taken in average. The percentage of total workers to total population in villages with AWR is 49.64 per cent while it is 48.48 per cent for the case of villages without AWR. Moreover, the percentage of main workers to total workers in the former is 89.13 per cent while in the latter, main workers compose 83.60 per cent of the total workers.

The percentage of marginal workers is higher in villages with poor road connectivity. This can be taken to denote the undeveloped state of agriculture through the mirror of mass practice of unsustainable shifting cultivation, which is mostly seasonal in nature. In the villages connected with AWR, 5.83 per cent of the total workers are those who work for less than six months in a year while for villages without AWR connectivity, the percentage is 7.21.

The percentage of agricultural labourers is higher in villages with better road connectivity. In relation to the total number of workers, the average percentage of agricultural labourers in villages connected with AWR is 8.58 per cent while for the unconnected, it is 4.42 per cent. Also, the ratio of agricultural labourers in villages along the main route is significantly higher at 12.41 per cent while the same is only 4.98 per cent for villages outside the main route. It may be hypothesised that the problem of land availability has emerged as a result of road connectivity, especially in the areas along the main transport route. Lands in these villages with better connectivity attract wealthy investors, which in turn raises the price of such lands. So, workers have to work in other people's farms thus becoming agricultural labourers.

It was also found that there are more cultivators in villages with poor road connectivity. Their percentage in total number of workers is 82.93 per cent in villages not connected with AWR and in villages with AWR connectivity, the percentage is 75.02. On the other hand, although still at a low level in both categories of workers, a greater contribution of industrial activities was found among the main and marginal workers of villages with better road connectivity. 0.55 per cent of main workers are household industry workers in villages connected with AWR while its counterpart showed 0.47 per cent only. At the same time, 3.07 per cent of marginal workers of villages with AWR are household industry workers while in villages not connected with AWR, the percentage is 2.74.

Examination of the existing state of land utilisation for determining the status of agricultural development shows that the area of wet rice cultivation (WRC) is higher in villages with better road connectivity. In villages connected with AWR, the percentage of WRC to total area of village is higher at 0.85 while for those not connected with it, it is 0.83 per cent.

Agricultural plantation area is also higher in villages with better road connectivity. It was found that 0.31 per cent of these villages are areas under plantation. On the other hand, the percentage for unconnected villages is only 0.09. The fact that agricultural plantation area is higher in the former denotes a favourable state of agriculture as it is a viable option when the topography of the state is taken into consideration.

The percentage of forest area to the total area of the village was found to be higher in villages that are poorly connected. In AWR-connected villages, the percentage is 73.88 but in those not connected, the percentage of forest area is 76.27. Moreover, the jhum size per family was also found to be higher in the villages with poor road connectivity. The jhum size in villages not connected with AWR is 4.36 hectares while in villages connected with AWR, it is 3.44 hectares. This points to the fact that jhumming is practised at a more extensive level in the poorly connected villages.

The geographical area of the well-connected villages was found to be larger than the poorly connected ones. The average area of villages connected with AWR is 37.86 sq. km while that of unconnected villages is 36.43 sq. km. Moreover, the area within one km from motorable road was also found to be significantly higher in the villages with better road connectivity. The area for AWR-connected villages is 11.73 sq. km while for unconnected villages, it is 2.98 sq. km.

In most of the cases, the connected villages show higher availability of educational facilities and more favourable achievement in their personnel, which are respectively measured through the number of schools per village and the teacher-pupil ratio. The average number of schools, primary to higher secondary schools, is 5.48 for villages connected with AWR but for those not connected with it, the average is 3.42. At the same time, in AWR-connected villages, there are 10.11 teachers per 100 students while for villages not connected with AWR, there are 9.49 teachers per 100 students.

Analysis of the average number of health care facilities like Community Health Centres, Primary Health Centres, Sub-Centres, and Sub-Centre Clinics and the average number of doctors, nurses, and health workers per 1000 population shows a higher performance in villages with better road connectivity. Out of the total villages that are connected with AWR, 68.89 per cent have health facilities at least of some type while for those that are not connected with AWR, the percentage of the same is 52.22 per cent. Furthermore, in the measure of the availability of drinking water supply, the villages with better road connectivity also showed better performance. With an overall average of 32.58 litres per capita per day (LPCD), the AWR-connected villages enjoy 33.79 LPCD while the unconnected have an LPCD of 31.27.

Analytical Results of the Impact of Road Connectivity on Rural Development

The t-test for the significance of differences between the villages with better road connectivity and poor road connectivity showed that there is a significant difference between the two areas in most of the key development parameters where the former is endowed with more favourable conditions. In the test of demographic status, the t-statistic was found to be significant in most of the cases except population density, sex ratio, and child sex ratio. As it was observed that villages with superior road connectivity showed better situations, it can be concluded that road connectivity leads to significant differences between villages with better road connectivity and those with poor connectivity statuses while at the same time favouring the former.

The result of estimated regression of population quality on road connectivity showed that the coefficients of AWR connectivity are significant in most of the cases. The positively significant coefficient implicates increasing population size, sex ratio, number of households, literacy rate, and female literacy rate with AWR connection. At the same time, a negatively significant coefficient suggests a decline in child-population ratio with AWR connectivity of the village. It can thus be concluded that population development is directly associated with AWR connectivity by taking low dependency ratio (child-population ratio) as one of the development parameters.

The study observed the situation where the composition of employment (workers' composition) is barely impacted by road connectivity in most of the cases. However, an interesting observation is the increase of agricultural labourers with better connectivity situations, which suggests the existence of land scarcity where the poor landless suffer. In the t-test, the statistics for the percentage of agricultural labourers of main and marginal workers were found to be significant in AWR connectivity and Main Route classifications. At the same time, the regression model showed a significant estimate for agricultural labourers (marginal) in the AWR connectivity classification. This may imply two things. First, scarcity of land for jhumming which compels many workers to work in other landowners' farm, and second, the practice of shifting cultivation as a mere subsidiary livelihood in the villages connected with AWR.

The estimated regression of the composition of workers on AWR connectivity also showed a negatively significant percentage of cultivators among main workers, which can be taken to imply the situation that shifting cultivation remains to be the main provider of employment in the poorly connected villages. In addition, it was found that the percentage of workers to total population and agricultural labourers increased with increasing road density; and that the percentage of main workers decreased while that of marginal workers increased with increasing distance from AWR.

With respect to the status of agricultural development, the study observed a higher prevalence of settled cultivation in the form of agricultural plantation in the well-connected villages whereas jhumming is practised more extensively in unconnected villages. The t-statistics were found to be significant for both these cases in AWR connectivity and Main Route classifications while Road Network showed a significant difference between its categories in the percentage of agricultural plantation area. Moreover, the sign of the regression coefficients implicates the increasing trends of plantation areas with connectivity improvement and at the same time, the increase in jhum size with poor connectivity. The analysis found a positive coefficient for agricultural plantation area and a negative coefficient for average jhum size per household. This result shows the practice of agricultural plantation at a more intense level in villages connected by AWR and the increase in jhum size per household for villages not connected with AWR, which relatively have smaller geographical area.

The study observed a situation where the well connected villages are better endowed with educational infrastructure and manpower (teachers). The t-test showed that the number of schools is significantly higher in all levels of schooling in such villages. However, the test for teacher-student ratio showed significant differences in high schools and higher secondary schools only. At the same time, coefficients of the estimated regression of educational institutions on AWR connectivity were found to be significant for the availability of schools at various levels while for Road Network, it was found to be significant at all levels. The other estimated regression, i.e., educational personnel on road connectivity showed that the coefficient of AWR connectivity is significant for high schools while that of Road Network is significant for middle, high, and higher secondary schools. This shows that although the availability of these educational facilities are more or less the same in the two areas for primary education, the availability for middle school and above is significantly higher in the connected villages than in the unconnected ones.

The chi-square test showed that the value for the availability of health care institutions is significant at all levels. This level of significance and its sign mean that there are more health care facilities available in villages with better road connectivity than in villages with poor road connectivity. In other words, the average performance of villages having better connectivity conditions is significantly higher with respect to the availability of the various health care facilities.

Another notable feature is the significantly different number of qualified medical staff between the well-connected and poorly connected villages. The t-statistic was found to be significantly higher in the villages with better road connectivity for total number of doctors and nurses. At the same time, the estimated regression showed that the coefficients of AWR connectivity and Road Network for doctors and nurses are significant. The availability of doctors and nurses in the well-connected villages being significantly higher gives confidence to the conclusion that well-connected villages have a better performance in terms of medical care.

Conclusion and Recommendations

In spite of the fact that there are various factors at play that lead to spatial patterns of development set up across the different villages of Mizoram, the analysis observed clear distinction in the indicators of economic development among the villages that possesses different connectivity status. This can be seen from the significantly different performances between the categories of villages in the various development indicators like child-population ratio, family size, literacy rates, percentage of total workers, agricultural plantation area, jhum area, and in the availability of basic social infrastructures viz., education and health care. In addition, taking the sign of regression coefficient as the mode in which road connectivity impacted development (whether positively or negatively), it can be stated that road connectivity does have a direct bearing on economic development in the study areas.

The estimated regression equation showed a positively significant coefficient for agricultural plantation while a negatively significant coefficient was observed for jhum size. It may thus be concluded that road connectivity significantly increases agricultural plantation area while it has a negative impact on the intensity of jhum practice. Likewise, the significant coefficient for literacy implicates increasing literacy rate with road connectivity. In addition, the study observed a significantly increasing percentage of main workers while also observing increasing percentage of agricultural labourers with road connectivity.

Although the R-square of the estimated regression model is comparatively low, the significance of the calculated F-statistic with low presence of multicollinearity can be interpreted as a model where the explanatory (road connectivity) variables undoubtedly have a significant impact on the dependent (development) variables. It should be noted that the explanatory variables introduced in the model may be one group of significant factors among others; while the possibility of a sequential process in the impact of road connectivity on development cannot be ruled out. Nevertheless, based on the significance of estimated regression, it is safe to conclude that road connectivity is a significant factor for economic development in rural areas.

In light of the findings of the study, there are some key issues that need to be addressed to achieve sustained rural development in the state. They are given as follows:

a) The extreme dependence of the state on central government for the enhancement of road connectivity, as indicated by a higher percentage of surfaced national highways and the declining budget allocation for roads, should be a matter of concern. Moreover, the state's own roads like village and town roads are in a deplorable state and the majority of them are still unsurfaced. Keeping in view the impact of road connectivity noted above, it is considered necessary that more effort be given by the state government towards the provision of this public good.

b) The study did not find active participation of the community in the construction and maintenance of rural roads. The villagers themselves should be considered the true stakeholders in this and so, it is necessary to evolve strategies to include the people especially in building and in the maintenance of roads like internal and agriculture link roads.

c) The increasing percentage of agricultural labourers in well-connected villages should be a matter of concern. In fact, the study observed large (average) area of jhum cultivation in the villages. It is thus recommended that measures to minimise the prevalent practice of shifting the cultivation from one tract of land to the other be forwarded, so that the current landless agriculture labourers could exploit such lands for cultivation.

d) Health infrastructure was found to be significantly inadequate in poorly connected villages, which thwart the goal of universal health care coverage. This differing availability should be positively addressed by the state government. Keeping in view the provisions of the Directive Principles of State Policy, even the remotest of the villages should be provided these facilities. This also holds true for the case of educational infrastructures.

e) The significant estimated regression coefficient of AWR connectivity on availability of schools and teacher-student ratio for middle school, high school, and higher secondary school should be a matter of concern because its unavailability in the poorly connected villages could result in discontinuation of schooling after the students had completed the primary level.

f) The practice of jhum cultivation is done at a more intense level in villages with poor road connectivity, the reason for which may be the absence of alternative livelihood options. At the same time, the study found that jhumming is still practised in the well connected areas where agriculture plantation is being underraken at a larger extent. This means that jhum cultivation is practised in the villages of Mizoram irrespective of whether they are well-connected or not, although at a lesser degree in the former. Focusing on not only the environmental effect of jhum cultivation but also on how hard it is for the people to completely move away from it, efficient measures to regulate and control the intensity of jhum practice are indispensable.

g) The significantly positive relationship between road density and agriculture plantation area points to the fact that the success of agricultural plantation transpires with the increasing road density or vice versa. Thus, it is necessary that larger road density, especially agricultural link roads, be created in the villages for further expansion of agricultural plantation area – which is considered to be the main alternative for jhum practice.

The exercise and observations of the analysis of road connectivity on rural development suggest the need for further research in some specific areas. The following are the areas found to be relatively important:

i) As cited earlier, the percentage of agricultural labourers rises with road connectivity which clearly shows that connectivity leads to changes in land ownership. This calls for a study focusing on how road connectivity affects existing land relation in rural areas. To elaborate, road connectivity often leads to the emergence of market for land. Moreover, enhanced communication through road connectivity allows the urban rich to access such lands thus raising the value of lands along the roadside. The poor villagers would sell their land because of one reason or the other to these buyers and in the end, this results in a new form of land relation. This also leads to a rise in the number of agricultural labourers as the villagers without other livelihood options can now only serve as labourers in other people's farms. It is necessary to undergo a research that studies the causes of such morphology of land relation and rise in agricultural labourers because it has been experienced that alienation of land had led to social uprisings such as the Naxalism movement and the like.
ii) The findings of the study note that jhumming is not only done at an intensive level in the remote villages but also in the well-connected villages, although at a lesser intensity. Further research is necessary to study the extent to which the residents of these villages are dependent on this practice and also in finding ways to make the current practice more sustainable.
iii) Analysis of the existing data sets revealed that there is a change in the socio-economic condition of the villages with improvements in road connectivity. However, what is perceptible is that there is endogeneity in the development process and so, a more intensive research is called for to study which key variable(s) is being affected foremost by road connectivity and how that key variable has impacts on other development variables. Moreover, due to limited availability of data, some indicators of quality of life like infant mortality rate, school dropouts, maternal mortality, etc. were not covered in the study. It is considered necessary to study whether these indicators are sensitive to road connectivity and / or to the lack of it.
iv) The study proved that road connectivity leads to favourable changes in the agricultural scenario of the state as agricultural plantation area rises and jhum area falls with improvements in connectivity. However, the present

data set lacked certain variables like agricultural value chain which may have a susceptible relationship with road transport. Therefore, an analysis of the impact of roads and road transport on such a chain of agricultural marketing could provide a deeper understanding of how enhancement in road connectivity affects the agricultural sector.

Bibliography

Abrams, Steve (2013), *The Unseen History of Our Roads*, Online, Extracted from http://www.roadandtrack.com/car-culture/a4447/the-road-ahead-road evolution/ on 28.10.2015 at 11:18 PM.

ADB (2002), *Impact of Rural Roads on Poverty Reduction: A Case Study-Based Analysis*, Asian Development Bank, October 2002.

Adedeji, O.A., E.M. Olafiaji, F.K. Omole, J.A. Olanibi and Yusuff Lukman (2014), 'An Assessment of the Impact of Road Transport on Rural Development: A Case Study of Obokun Local Government Area of Osun State, Nigeria,' *British Journal of Environmental Sciences*, Vol.2, No. 1, pp. 34-48, European Centre for Research Training and Development, UK.

Adelman, Irma (1961), *Theories of Economic Growth and Development*, Stanford University Press, California.

Aderamo, A.J. and S.A. Magaji, S. A. (2010). 'Rural transportation and the distribution of public facilities in Nigeria: Case study of Edu Local Government Area of Kwara State,' *Journal of Human Ecology*, 29(3): 171-179.

Affum, Joseph and Farhad Ahmed (1995), *Use of GIS as a Decision Making Tool in Integrated Rural Transport Planning*, University of South Australia.

Aggarwal, Shilpa (2013), *Do Rural Roads Create Pathways out of Poverty? Evidence from India*, Online, Extracted from http://www.isb.edu/faculty/ shilpa_aggarwal/files/shilpa-aggarwal-rural-roads.pdf on 14.8.2015 at 11:31 PM.

Ahmed, Sadia E., Carlos M. Souza, Júlia Riberio, and Robert M. Ewers (2013) 'Temporal Patterns of Road Network Development in the Brazilian Amazon,' in *Regional Environmental Change*, Springer.

Ajram, Kasem (1992), *The Miracle of Islam Science* (2nd Ed.), Knowledge House Publishers, Michigan.

Alba, Carlos A and Edward Beimborn (2004), *Relationship Between Land Use Patterns and Highway Widening*, Centre for Urban Transportation Studies, University of Winsconsin, Milwaukee, Online, Extracted from https://www4.uwm.edu/cuts/lu/carlos.pdf on 13.5.2015 at 01:05 PM.

Angelsen, A. (1999) 'Agricultural Expansion and Deforestation: Modeling the Impact of Population, Market Forces and Property Rights' *Journal of Development Economics* 58(1): 185-218.

APERP (1997), '*Rural Transport Survey 1997*' – Andhra Pradesh Economic Restructuring Project, World Bank, Washington DC.

Appu, P.S. (1974), 'Agrarian Structure and Rural Development,' *Economic and Political Weekly*, Vol. 9, No. 39, pp. A70-A75, Sameeksha Trust.

Arthur, Jones Lewis (2005) *Family Size and its Socio-Economic Implication in the Sunyani Municipality of the Brong Ahafo Region of Ghana, West Africa*, Centre for Development Studies, University of Cape Coast, Ghana.

Aschauer, D.A. (1989), 'Is Public Expenditure Productive?' *Journal of Monetary Economics*, 23, pp. 177–200.

Atagher, Monica Mwuese and Deborah Maanenge Atagher (2014), 'Assessment of the Availability of Rural Infrastructure, Agriculture Credit and Cooking Fuel among Project and Non-Project Farmers in Benue State, Nigeria, *Journal of Agriculture and Veterinary Science (ISOR-JAVS)*, Vol. 7, Issue 11 Ver. III (Nov.), pp. 17-22, ISOR.

Banerjee, Rakesh and Ashish Sachdeva (2015) 'Pathways to Preventive Health, Evidence from India's Rural Road Program,' *USC-INET Research Paper No. 15-19*, Online, Extracted from SSRN: http://ssrn.com/abstract=2636999 or http://dx.doi.org/10.2139/ ssrn.2636999 on 21/10/2015 at 11:00 PM

Barwell, I and Jonathan Dawson (1993), *Roads Are Not Enough: New Perspectives on Rural Transport Planning in Developing Countries*, I.T. Publications, London.

Barwell, I, G.A. Edmonds, J.D.G.F Howe and J de Veen (1985), *Rural Transport in Developing Countries*, Intermediate Technology Publications and Boulder, London.

Bell, Clive (2010), *Goods, Education and Health: A Combined Model for Evaluating PMGSY*, University of Heidelberg, Germany.

Bhandari, Laveesh and Siddhartha Dutta (2007), 'Health Infrastructure in Rural India,' *India Infrastructure Report 2007*, pp. 265-285, Oxford University Press, New Delhi.

Bhatt, Bindu and Janak P Joshi (2013), 'A Geospatial Approach for Assessing and Modeling Spatial Accessibility of the Primary Health Centers in the Tribal Talukas of the Vadodara District,' *International Journal of Gromatics and Geosciences*' Vol. 3, No. 3, pp. 582-591.

Bhattacharya, Prabir C (2012), 'Gender Inequality and the Sex Ratio in Three Emerging Economies,' Heriot-Watt University, Department of Economics, *Working Paper No. 2012-01*, Edinburgh, UK.

Binswanger, Hans P., S. R. Khandker and M. R. Rosenzweig (1989), 'How Infrastructure and Financial Institutions Affect Agriculture Output and Investment in India,' *Policy Planning and Research Working Paper* No.163, World Bank, Washington D.C.

Boserup, Ester (1976), 'Environment, Population and Technology in Primitive Societies,' *Population and Development Review*, Vol. 2, No. 1 (March), pp. 21-36, Population Council.

Bourdet, Y. (1998), 'The Dynamics of Regional Disparities in Laos: The Poor and The Rich,' *Asian Survey* 38, 629–652.

Bravo, Ana (2002), 'The Impact of Improved Rural Roads on Gender Relations in Peru,' *Mountain Research and Development*, Vol. 22, No. 3, pp. 221-224, International Mountain Society.

Button, Kenneth (2010), *Transport Economics*, 3rd Edition, Edward Elgar Publishing Limited, UK.

Button, Kenneth (1998), 'Infrastructure Investment, Endogenous Growth and Economic Convergence', *The Annals of Regional Science*, 32, pp. 145-162.

Canning D. and E. Bennathan (2000), 'The Social Rate of Returns on Infrastructure Investment,' *Policy Research Working Paper Series* 2390, World Bank, Washington DC.

Castaing, Marie Gachassin (2011), *Education and Road Connectivity: Empirical Evidence from Tanzania*, Centre d'Economie de la Sorbonne, Universite Paris 1, 106-112.

Census of India (2011), *Provisional Population Totals*, Office of the Registrar General and Census Commissioner, Government of India.

Chalamwong, Y. and Feder, G. (1988). 'The Impact of Land Ownership Security: Theory and Evidence from Thailand,' *World Bank Economic Review*, Vol. 2, pp. 187-204.

Chambers, Robert (2006), *Poverty Unperceived: Traps, Biases and Agenda*, Institute of Development Studies, University of Sussex, Brighton, UK.

Chaudhary, S.K. (2012), 'Innovative Construction Technology for Quality Construction of Rural Road' *The Masterbuilder*, August 2012 issue, pp.88-94.

Chauhan, Abhishek (2014), 'Need for Rural Development in India for Nation Building,' *Asian Mirror – International Journal of Research*, Vol. 1, Issue 1, February 2014, pp.1-8.

Chomitz, Kenneth M and David A. Gray (1996), 'Roads, Land Use, and Deforestation: A Spatial Model Applied to Belize,' *The World Bank Economic Review*, Vol. 10, No. 3, pp. 487-512, Oxford University Press.

CIA (2014), 'Country Comparisons: Roadways,' *The World Factbook* (2013-14 Edition), Central Intelligence Agency, United States, Online, Extracted from https://www.cia.gov/library/publications/the-world-factbook/rankorder/raw data_2085.txt on 25/11/2015 at 12:48 AM

Copeland, Claudia, Linda Levine and William J. Mallett (2011), *The Role of Public Works Infrastructure in Economic Recovery,* Online, Extracted from https://www.fas.org/sgp/crs/misc/R42018.pdf on 18/9/2015 at 11:43 PM.

Copus, Andrew, Peter Weingarten, Christian Lindner, Gerd Eiden, Ronald McQuaid, Malcolm Greig and Mats Johansson (2006), '*Study on Employment in Rural Areas,*' European Commission, Belgium.

Creightney, Cavelle D. (1993), 'Transport and Economic Performance: A Survey of Developing Countries,' *World Bank Technical Paper 232*, Washington, D.C.

Cypher, James M. and James L. Dietz (2004), *The Process of Economic Development*, 2nd Edition, Routledge, London.

Deininger, Klaus and John Okidi (2003), 'Growth and Poverty Reduction in Uganda, 1999-200: Panel Data Evidence,' *Development Policy Review*, 21 (4), pp. 481-509, Blackwell Publishing, Oxford, UK.

Deller, Steven C and Carl H. Nelson (1991), 'Measuring the Economic Efficiency of Producing Rural Road Services,' *American Journal of Agricultural Economics*, Vol. 73, No. 1 (Feb., 1991), pp. 194-201, Oxford University Press.

Desmet, Klaus and Esteban Rossi-Hansberg (2014), 'Spatial Development,' *American Economic Review 2014,* Vol. 104 No. 4, pp. 1211-1243.

Diamond, Jared (2005), *Collapse: How Societies Choose to Fail or Succeed*, Penguin Group, New York, USA.

Diener, Ed and Eunkook Suh (1997), 'Measuring Quality of Life: Economic, Social and Subjective Indicators' *Social Indicators Research*, 40, pp. 189-216, Kiuwer Academic Publishers, Netherlands.

Dorosh, Paul, Hyoung-Gun Wang, Liangzhi You, Emily Schmidt (2012), 'Road connectivity, population, and crop production in Sub-Saharan Africa,' *Agricultural Economics 43* (2012), pp. 89–103, International Association of Agricultural Economists.

Dorosh, P., H.G. Wang, L. You and E. Schmidt (2009) *Crop Production and Road Connectivity in Sub-Saharan Africa: A Spatial Analysis*, The International Bank for Reconstruction and Development: The World Bank, Washington, DC.

Drummond, H. Evan and John W. Goodwin (2004), *Agricultural Economics*, Second Edition, Pearson Education, Delhi.

Economic Survey (2014-15), Department of Economic Affairs, Ministry of Finance, Government of India.

Edmonds, G. (1998), *Wasted Time: The Price of Poor Access*, Development Policies Department, International Labor Organization, Geneva.

Ellis, S.D. (1997), *Key Issues in Rural Transport in Developing Countries*, TRL Report, Overseas Development Administration, London.

Essang, S.M. and AF Mabamonku (1975), 'Impact of Urban Migration on Rural Development: Theoretical Considerations and Empirical Evidence from Southern Nigera,' *The Developing Economies*, Volume 13, Issue 2, pp 137-149.

Eze, S.O. (2012), 'Assessment of the Impact of Rural Infrastructures (Water Supply and Feeder Roads) by Ebonyi State Agricultural Development Programme (EBADEP) on Farmers Agricultural Practices and Socio-Economic Status,' *International Journal of Advanced Biological Research*, Vol. 2 (3), pp. 515-521, Society for Science and Nature.

Faiz, Asif (2012), *The Promise of Rural Roads: Review of the Role of Low-Volume Roads in Rural Connectivity, Poverty Reduction, Crisis Management and Livability*, Transportation Research Circular, Washington D.C.

Faiz, Asif, Aysha Faiz, Wei Wang and Christopher Bennett (2012), 'Sustainable Rural Roads for Livelihoods and Livability,' *Procedia – Social and Behavioral Sciences* 53, pp. 1-8, Elsevier Ltd.

Fajardo, Feliciano R (1994), *Economic Development*, Third Edition, National Book Store, Manila, Philippines.

Fan, Shenggen., Peter Hazell and S. K. Thorat (2000), 'Impact of Public Expenditure on Poverty in Rural India,' *Economic and Political Weekly*, 30 September, 35, pp. 3581-3588.

Farole, Thomas (2012), 'Competitiveness and Connectivity: Integrating Lagging Regions in Global Markets,' *Economic Premise*, October, No. 93, Poverty Reduction and Economic Management Network, World Bank.

Freitas, Simone R., Todd J. Hawbaker and Jean Paul Metzger (2009), 'Effects of Roads, Topography, and Land Use on Forest Cover Dynamics in the Brazilian Atlantic Forestm' *Forest Ecology and Management* 259, (2010) pp. 410-417.

Gachassin, Maria, Boris Najman and Gael Raballand (2010), 'The Impact of Roads on Poverty Reduction: A Case Study of Cameroon,' *Policy Research Working Paper 5209*, The World Bank Africa Region Transport Unit, February 2010.

Gill, Zufiqar Ahmad, Khalid Mustafa, Waqar Ahmad Jehangir and Muhammad Ali (1999), 'Rural Development in the 21st Century: Some Issues' *The Pakistan Development Review*, Vol. 38, No. 4, pp 1177-1190, Pakistan Institute of Development Economics, Islamabad.

Goel, Deepika (2003), 'Impact of Infrastructure on Productivity: Case of Indian Registered Manufacturing,' *Indian Economic Review*, New Series, Vol. 38, No. 1 (January-June 2003), pp. 95-113, Department of Economics, Delhi School of Economics, University of Delhi.

Gollin, Douglas (2010), *Agriculture, Roads and Economic Development in Uganda*, NBER Working Paper 15863, National Bureau of Economic Research, Cambridge, MA.

Golmohammadi, Farhood (2012), 'Rural Roads, Sustainable Development and Maintenance of People in Desert Regions; Case Study: South Khorasan Province - East of Iran,' *International Journal of Science and Engineering Investigations*, Vol. 1, Issue 9, October 2012, pp. 118-133.

Gujarati, Damodar N, Dawn C Porter and Sangeetha Gunasekar (2012), *Basic Econometrics*, Tata McGraw Hill Education (India) Private Limited, New Delhi.

Hansen, W. G. (1959), 'How Accessibility Shapes Land Use,' *Journal of American Planning Institute*, Vol. 25, pp. 73–76.

Henriques, Pedro D. S., Vanda Narciso and Manuel Branco (2011), *The Role of Traditional Land Use Systems in the Well-Being of Rural Timor-Leste*, CEFAGE-UE Working Paper 2011/08, Center for Advanced Studies in Management and Economics of the Universidade de Évora

Hesselbarth, Susanne (2005), *Socio-Economic Impacts of Water Supply and Sanitation Projects*, Online, Extracted from https://www.kfw-entwicklungsbank.de/migration/ Entwicklungsbank-Startseite/Entwicklungs finanzierung/Sektoren/Wasser/ Engagement-der-KfW-Entwicklungsbank/ Wirkungen.pdf on 17/5/2015 at 10:43 PM.

Hirschman, Charles (1981), 'The Uses of Demography in Development Planning,' *Economic Development and Cultural Change*, Vol. 29, No. 3, The University of Chicago, USA.

Howe, John and Peter Richards (1984), *Rural Roads and Poverty Alleviation*, Intermediate Technology Publications and Boulder, London.

Huang, Shu-Wei and Hsui-I Hsieh (2014), 'The Study of the Relationship between Accessibility and Mixed Land Use in Tainan, Taiwan,' *International Journal of Environmental Science and Development*, Vol. 5, No. 4, August 2014, pp. 352-356.

Hull, Katy (2009), 'Understanding the Relationship between Economic Growth, Employment and Poverty Reduction,' *Promoting Pro-Poor Growth: Employment*, OECD.

Ibok, Enefiok and Ekong Daniel (2013), 'The Impact of Rural Roads and Bridges on the Socio-Economic Development of Akwa Ibom State, Nigeria: An Evaluation,' *Global Journal of Political Science and Administration*, Vol.1, No.1, pp. 27-36, September 2013, European Centre for Research Training and Development.

Ibrahim, Sa'ad (2013), 'Comparing Alternative Methods of Measuring Geographic Access to Health Services: An Assessment of People's Access to Specialist Hospital in Kebbi State,' *Academic Journal of Interdisciplinary Studies*, Vol. 2, No. 12, November 2013, pp. 109-116, MCSER Publishing, Rome.

Ikejiofor, Ijeoma Gladys and Alphosus Ali (2014), 'The Effects of Road Transport Characteristics on the Marketing of Agricultural Produce in Nssuka LGA, Enugu State, Southeastern Nigeria,' *Innovare Journal of Social Sciences*, Vol. 2, Issue 1, 2014.

Jacobson, Herbert Reinhold (1940), *A History of Roads from Ancient Times to the Motor Age*, M.Sc. Thesis, Georgia School of Technology, Atlanta.

Jacoby, H.G. (2000) 'Access to Markets and the Benefits of Rural Roads,' *The Economic Journal 110*, pp. 713–737, Royal Economic Society.

Jacoby, H.G. and Bart Minten (2008), 'On Measuring the Benefits of Lower Transport Costs,' *World Bank Working Paper*, 4484, World Bank.

Jalan, J., and M. Ravallion, (2002) 'Geographic Poverty Traps? A Micro Model of Consumption Growth in Rural China,' *Journal of Applied Econometrics,* 17(4), pp. 329-46.

Joshi, B.M. (1990), *Infrastructure and Economic Development in India,* Ashish Publishing House, New Delhi.

Khandker, Shahidur R., Zaid Bakht, Gayatri B. Koolwal (2006), 'The Poverty Impact of Rural Roads: Evidence from Bangladesh,' *World Bank Policy Research Working Paper 3875*, April 2006, World Bank.

Kingombe, Christian (2011), *Achieving Pro-Poor Growth through Investment in Rural Feeder Roads: The Role of Impact Evaluation*, Background Note, August 2011, Overseas Development Institute, London.

Kiprono, Philemon and Tomoya Matsumoto (2014), *Roads and Farming: The Effect of Infrastructure Improvement on Agricultural Input Use, Farm Productivity and Market Participation in Kenya*, CSAE Conference: Economic Development in Africa, University of Oxford.

Kularatne, C (2006), *Social and Economic Infrastructure Impacts on Economic Growth in South Africa*, Presented at the UCT School of Economics Staff Seminar Series, October 2006.

Kumar, Anand (2015), 'Infrastructure: Key for Development of the North-East,' *Yojana*, Vol. 59, pp. 37-39, November 2015.

Kwon, E.K. (2000), *Infrastructure, Growth, and Poverty Reduction in Indonesia: A Cross-sectional Analysis*, Asian Development Bank, Manila.

Levinson, David and Arthur Huang (2012), 'A Positive Theory of Network Connectivity,' *Environment and Planning B: Planning and Design 2012,* Vol. 39, pp. 308-325.

Lipton, M (2005), 'Urban Bias,' in Forsyth, T. (ed) *Encyclopedia of International Development*, Routledge, London.

Lipton, Michael and Martin Ravallion (1995), 'Poverty and Policy,' in J. Behrman and T.N. Srinivasan (Eds.) *Handbook of Development Economics III*, Elsevier, New York.

Litman, Todd and Rowan Steele (2015), *Land Use Impacts on Transport: How Land Use Factors Affect Travel Behavior*, Online, Extracted from http://www.vtpi.org/landtravel.pdf on 11/8/2015 at 11:14 PM

Llanto, Gilberto M. (2012), 'The Impact of Infrastructure on Agricultural Productivity,' *Phillipine Institute for Development Studies* Discussion Paper Series No. 2012-12.

Lokshin, Michael and Ruslan Yemstov (2005), 'Has Rural Infrastructure Rehabilitation in Georgia Helped the Poor?' *The World Bank Economic Review*, Vol. 19, No. 2 (2005), pp. 311-333, Oxford University Press.

Lombard, P and L Coetzer (2006), *The Estimation of the Impact of Rural Road Investments on Socio-Economic Development*, Online, Extracted from http://roadsforwater.org/wp-content/uploads/2013/11/Estimating-the-Impact-of-Road-Inv-on-SocioEcon-Development.pdf on 12/7/2015 at 11:56 PM.

Lutz, Wolfgang and Samir K.C. (2014), *Demography and Human Development: Education and Population Projections*, United Nations Development Programme, Occasional Paper 2013/04.

MacPherson, Yvonne (2007) 'Images and Icons: Harnessing the Power of Media to Reduce Sex-Selective Abortion in India,' *Gender and Development* 15 (2), November, pp. 413–23.

Manjah, Frankie Bendindang (2005), *The Socio-Economic Impact of Roads on Rural Communities, A Case Study of the Longhouses Communities of Rumah Ukan, Rumah Jandok and Rumah Bundong of Ulu Bukit Guram-Ulu Yong Road*, Master of Environment Management (Development Planning) Dissertation, University Malaysia Sarawak.

Mankiw, N Gregory (2014), *Essential of Economics*, Seventh Edition, Cengage Learning, Stamford, USA.

Masood, Muhammah Tahir, Azhar Khan, Hasnain A. Naqvi (2011) 'Transportation Problems in Developing Countries Pakistan: A Case-in-Point,' *International Journal of Business and Management*, Vol. 6, No. 11, Canadian Center of Science and Education, Toronto.

Mizoram Economic Survey (2014-15), Planning & Programme Implementation Department, Government of Mizoram.

Mohapatra, J.K. and B.P. Chandrasekhar (2007), *Rural Roads*, Online, Extracted from http://www.iitk.ac.in/3inetwork/html/reports/IIR2007/05-Rural%20Roads.pdf on 10/12/2015 at 11:27 PM.

MoHRD (1998), *National Policy on Education 1986 (As Modified in 1992)*, Department of Education, Ministry of Human Resource Development, Government of India, New Delhi.

MoRD (2015), *Pradhan Mantri Gram Sadak Yojana: Programme Guidelines*, Ministry of Rural Development, Government of India, New Delhi.

MoRD (2000), *Empowerment of Rural India through Connectivity*, Ministry of Rural Development, Government of India, New Delhi.

Mostert, W.P (1985), 'Demography and Development,' *Development Southern Africa*, Volume 2, Issue 1, pp. 56-61.

Mu, Ren and Dominique van de Walle (2007), 'Rural Roads and Local Market Development in Vietnam,' *Policy Research Working Paper 4340*, The World Bank

Development Research Group, Human Development and Public Services Team, August 2007.

Munroe, D.K., J. Southworth and CM Tucker (2004), 'Modeling Spatially and Temporally Complex Land-Cover Change: The Case of Western Honduras,' *The Professional Geographer* 56, pp. 544–559.

NABARD (2004), *Infrastructure for Agriculture and Rural Development: An Impact Assessment of Investments in Rural Roads & Bridges under RIDF*, National Bank for Agriculture and Rural Development, Mumbai, India.

Nedozi, Fidelis O., Jude O. Obasanmi and J.A. Ighata (2014), 'Infrastructural Development and Economic Growth in Nigeria: Using Simultaneous Equation,' *J. Economics,* 5(3), pp. 325-332.

NHDP (2013), *National Highways Development Project: An Overview*, Government of India, New Delhi.

NITI Aayog (2015), *Comprehensive Roadmap for Development of North Eastern States and Similarly Positioned Eastern States of Bihar, Jharkhand, Chhatisgarh, Odisha and West Bengal,* National Institution for Transforming India Aayog, Government of India, New Delhi.

NTDPC (2014), *India Transport Report: Moving India to 2032*, Sandipan Deb (ed.), Routledge, New Delhi.

NTDPC (2013), *Roads and Road Transport,* National Transport Development Policy Committee, New Delhi: Transport Research Wing Ministry of Road Transport and Highways, Government of India.

OECD (2012), *Gender Equality in Education, Employment and Entrepreneurship*, Meeting of the OECD Council at Ministerial Level, May 2012, Paris.

Olagunju, F.I., O. Ayinde, M.O. Adewumi and G.B. Adesiji (2012), 'Effects of Rural Roads and Marketing Infrastructure on Income of Farming Households in Osun State – Implications for Sustainable Development,' *World Rural Observations* 2012, 4 (2), pp. 22-30.

Oraboune, Syviengxay (2008), *Infrastructure (Rural Road) Development and Poverty Alleviation in Lao PDR*, Institute of Developing Economies, Online, Extracted from http://www.ide.go.jp/English/Publish/Download/Dp/pdf/ 151.pdf on 20/10/2015 at 01:00 PM.

Pachuau, Rintluanga (2009), *Mizoram: A Study in Comprehensive Geography*, Northern Book Centre, New Delhi.

Palma, Andre de, Robin Lindsey, Emile Quinet, Roger Vickerman (eds.) (2011), *AHandbook of Transport Economics,* Edward Elgar Publishing Limited, UK.

Parida, Abash (2014) 'Role of Rural Road Connectivity (Pradhan Mantri Gram Sadk Yojana) in Accelerating Development & Improving Quality of Life,' in *International Journal of Innovative Research and Development,* September 2014, Vol. 3 Issue 9, pp. 67-72.

Parida, Abash (2014), 'Role of Rural Road Connectivity (PMGSY) in Improving Quality of Life in Odisha,' *Odisha Review*, November 2014, pp.63-68.

Perz, Stephen G, Alexander Shenkin, Grenville Barnes, Liliana Cabrera, Lucas A. Carvalho and Jorge Castillo (2011), 'Connectivity and Resilience: A Multidimensional

Analysis of Infrastructure Impacts in the Southwestern Amazon,' *Soc Indic Res 106*, pp. 259-285, Springer Science + Business Media B.V.

Population Reference Bureau (2011), *World Population Sheet Data*, Online, Extracted from http://www.prb.org/pdf11/2011population-data-sheet_eng.pdf on 1/6/ 2015 at 12:14 AM

Porter, Gina (2013), *Transport Services and Their Impact on Poverty and Growth in Rural Sub-Saharan Africa*, Africa Community Access Programme / Durham University.

Rajaraman, Indira (2005), 'Financing Rural Infrastructure in Developing Countries: The Case of India,' *Applied Econometrics and International Development*, Vol. 5-2, pp. 53-68, Euro-American Association of Economic Development.

Rao, K. Srinivas and K. Chandra Sekhar (2010), 'Rural Infrastructure: A Vital Ingredient for Double Digit Growth,' *Kurukshetra* Vol. 58, No. 10, pp. 3-8.

Rasmussen, Jens Erik Bendix and Eva Broegaard (2011), 'The Impact of Rural Transport on Socio-Economic Development in Nicaragua,' *Rural Transport*, IRF Bulletin Special Edition, Vol. 2, pp. 6-8, International Road Federation, Geneva.

Reynolds, D.J. (1961), 'The Economics of Rural Motorways,' *The Journal of Industrial Economics*, Vol. 10, No. 1, pp. 10-20, Wiley.

Rostow, W (1962), *The Process of Economic Growth*, 2nd Ed. Oxford University Press, New York.

Ruijsav, Arjan, Caspar Schweigmanb, Clemens Lutz (2004), 'The Impact of Transport- and Transaction-Cost Reductions on Food Markets in Developing Countries: Evidence for Tempered Expectations for Burkina Faso. *Agricultural Economics*, 31, pp. 219-228.

Ryhal, Piar Chand and Shashi Punam (2009), 'A Study of Human Development Indicators and Decline Child Sex Ratio in Himachal Pradesh,' *The Journal of Family Welfare*, Vol. 55, No. 1, pp. 70-78.

Sahoo, Pravakar (2011), *Transport Infrastructure in India: Developments, Challenges and Lessons from Japan*, VRF Series No. 465, Institute of Developing Economies, Japan External Trade Organization.

Sarkar, Ashoke K. (2015), 'Issues and Challenges of Rural Roadways in India,' *Yojana*, Vol. 59, pp. 46-50, November 2015.

Sawmliana C and P. Pal Roy (2003), 'Importance of Slope Stability in Hilly Regions with Reference to Stone Quarrying in Mizoram' in *Proceedings: Geomechanics and Ground Control* by Satyendra K. Singh and Amalendu Sinha (eds.), Allied Publishers Pvt. Ltd., New Delhi

Scheidel, Walter (2006), 'Population and Democracy,' *Princeton/Stanford Working Papers in Classics*, Version 1.0, April 2006, Stanford University, USA.

Seshadri, V.S. (2014), *Transforming Connectivity Corridors between India and Myanmar into Development Corridors*, Research and Information System for Developing Countries, New Delhi.

Shah, A (1992), Public Infrastructure and Industrial Productivity, *Review of Economics and Statistics*, Vol. 74, pp.28-36.

Shah, Navinchandra R. (2013), 'Literacy Rate in India,' *International Journal of Reseach in all Subjects in Multi Languages*, Vol. 1, Issue 7, October 2013, pp. 12-16.

Shiferaw, Admasu, Mans Soderbom, Eyerusalem Siba, Getnet Alemu (2012), '*Road Infrastructure and Enterprise Development in Ethiopia*,' Working Paper, International Growth Centre, London. Online, Extracted from http://www.theigc.org/wp-content/uploads/2015/02/Shiferaw-Et-Al-2012-Working-Paper.pdf. on 19/10/2015 at 10:00 AM.

Singh, Katar (2009), *Rural Development: Principles, Policies and Management*, Third Edition, SAGE Publications, New Delhi.

Singh, Vidyapati (1962), 'Financing of Road Improvements for Farm Marketing,' *The Journal of Finance*, Vol. 17, No. 3, pp. 537-539.

Soares-Filho, B., A. Alencar, D. Nepstad, G. Cerqueira, M. del Carmen Vera Diaz, S. Rivero, L. Solorzano and E. Voll, (2004) 'Simulating the Response of Land-Cover Changes to Road Paving and Governance along a Major Amazon Highway: the Santarem-Cuiaba Corridor,' *Global Change Biology* 10, 745–764.

South, Scott J. and Katherine Trent (1988), 'Sex Ratios and Women's Role: A Cross-National Analysis,' *American Journal of Sociology*, 93, pp. 1096-1115.

Statistical Abstract of Mizoram (Various Issues), Directorate of Economics & Statistics, Government of Mizoram.

Statistical Handbook of Mizoram (Various Issues), Directorate of Economics & Statistics, Mizoram: Aizawl.

Sum, M. (2008), 'Infrastructure Development in Cambodia', in Kumar, N. (ed.), International Infrastructure Development in East Asia – Towards Balanced Regional Development and Integration, *ERIA Research Project Report 2007*-2, Chiba:IDE-JETRO, pp.32-84.

Talpur, Mir Aftab Hussain, Madzlan Napiah, Imtiaz Ahmad Chandio and Irfan Ahmed Memon (2014), 'Analyzing Public Sector Education Facilities: A Step Towards Accessible Basic Education Institutions in Destitute Subregions,' *International Eduction Studies,* Vol. 7, No. 4, pp. 110-119, Canadian Center for Science and Education.

TDM (Transport Demand Management) Encyclopedia (2015), *Roadway Connectivity: Creating More Connected Roadway and Pathway Networks*, Victoria Transport Policy Institute, Online, Extracted from http://www.vtpi.org/tdm/ tdm116.htm (Updated 15 April 2015) on 23/10/2015 at 08:00 PM.

Terefe, Lulit Aklilu (2012), *Impact of Road on Rural Poverty: Evidence from Fifteen Rural Villages in Ethiopia*, M.A. (Development Studies) Thesis, International Institute of Social Sciences.

Thanga, J.L.T. (2014), *The Study of Development and Management of Land and Water Resources for Sustainable Agriculture in Mizoram, India: Market Survey*, Japan International Cooperation Agency, Tokyo, Japan.

Thomas, Deborah (2001), *The Importance of Development Plans / Land Use Policy for Development Control*, Prepared for USAID/OAS Post-Georges Disaster Mitigation Project, Workshop for Building Inspectors, January 15-26, 2001.

Thomson, Elizabeth (2007), '*What is Demography?*' Online, Extracted from http://www.suda.su.se/docs/What%20is%20Demography.pdf on 20/10/2015 at 10:00 PM.

_______ (2015), 'Research in Population Studies,' *The Hindu*, January 5, 2015. Online, Extracted from http://www.thehindu.com/todays-paper/tp-miscellaneous/tpothers/research-in-population-studies/article6755422.ece on 02/10/2015 at 11:00 PM.

Todaro, Michael P. (1995), *Economic Development in the Third World,* 5th Edition, Longman, New York.

Todaro, Michael P. and Stephen C. Smith (2003), *Economic Development,* Eighth Edition, Pearson Education, Delhi.

Tunde, A.M. and E.E. Adeniyi (2012), 'Impact of Road Transport on Agricultural Development: A Nigerian Example,' *Ethiopian Journal of Environmental Studies and Management,* Vol. 5, No. 3, pp. 232-238.

Ulimwengu, John, Jose Funes, Derek Headey, Liang You (2009), *Paving the Way for Development: The Impact of Road Infrastructure on Agricultural Production and Household Wealth in the Democratic Republic of Congo,* Online, Extracted from http://www.unamur.be/en/eco/eeco/cred/working-papers-files/wp2012/workingpaper-2012-ulimwengu on 15/10/2015 at 02:00 PM

Umoren, V., I. Ema and A. Elijah (2012), 'Assessment of Road Development in Abak Local Government Area, Nigeria,' *Ethiopian Journal of Environmental Studies and Management,* Vol. 5, No. 4, pp. 324-331.

Umoren, V., E.E. Ikurekong, A. Emmanuel, A.A. Udida (2009), 'Development of Road Infrastructure as a Tool of Transforming Ibiono Ibom Local Government Area,' in *Global Journal of Social Sciences,* Vol. 8, No. 2, pp.53-59, Bachudo Science Co. Ltd, Nigeria.

United Nations (2012), *Macroeconomic Stability, Inclusive Growth and Employment: Thematic Think Piece,* Online, Extracted from http://www.un.org/ millenniumgoals/pdf/Think%20Pieces/12_macroeconomics.pdf on 25.8.2015 at 12:54 AM.

Van De Walle, Dominique (2002), 'Choosing Rural Road Investments to Help Reduce Poverty,' *World Development,* Vol. 30, No. 4, pp. 575–589, Elsevier Science Ltd, Great Britain.

Vargas, Paola (2007), *Connecting Rural Communities for Development: An Impact Evaluation of a Rural Roads Program in Peru,* 6th PEP Research Network General Meeting, Online, Extracted from http://www.pep-net.org/sites/pep-net.org/files/typo3doc/pdf/files_events/vargas-pa.pdf on 1/4/2015 at 11:30 PM.

Varshney, Ashutosh (1998), *Democracy, Development and the Countryside: Urban-Rural Struggles in India,* Cambridge University Press, New York.

Verma, RV (1980), 'Role of Periodic Markets in Integrated Area Development - A Case Study of Safipur Tehsil of Unnao District, U.P.,' *Transactions,* Vol. 8, Indian Council of Geographers.

Wills, Robert J. (1986) 'Wage Determinants: A Survey and Reinterpretation of Human Capital Earnings Functions.' *Handbook of Labor Economics,* Vol. 1, Chapter 10, pp. 525-602.

Windle, J. and R.A. Cramb (1997) 'Remoteness and Rural Development: Economic Impacts of Rural Roads on Upland Farmers in Sarawak, Malaysia,' *Asia Pacific Viewpoint,* 38, pp. 37–53, Blackwell Publishers, Oxford, UK.

Wood, Stanley, K. Sebastian, F. Nachtergaele, D. Nielsen, and A. Dai, (1999), 'Spatial Aspects of The Design and Targeting of Agricultural Development Strategies,' *Environment and Production Technology Division Discussion Paper* No. 44, International Food Policy Research Institute, Washington D.C.

World Bank (2014), *Rural Road Development in India: An Assessment of Distribution of PMGSY Project Benefits in Three States by Gender and Ascribed Social Groups*, Report No. AUS5487, South Asia Sustainable Development Unit, World Bank.

World Bank (2011), *Mizoram State Roads Project: Using Bioengineering to Stabilize Landslide-Prone Hillsides*, the World Bank in India.

World Bank (1994), *World Development Report 1994 – Infrastructure for Development*, World Bank, Washington D.C.

Yadav, Krishan K (2010), 'Road Connectivity as a Stimulant for Rural Poverty Reduction,' *Kurukshetra*, Vol. 58, No. 10, pp.12-15.

Index